FISHING FOR
A MAJOR

STUDENTS HELPING STUDENTS

FISHING FOR A MAJOR

NATAVI GUIDES, INC.

THE BERKLEY PUBLISHING GROUP
Published by the Penguin Group
Penguin Group (USA) Inc.
375 Hudson Street, New York, New York 10014, USA
Penguin Group (Canada), 10 Alcorn Avenue, Toronto, Ontario M4V 3B2, Canada
(a division of Pearson Penguin Canada Inc.)
Penguin Books Ltd., 80 Strand, London WC2R 0RL, England
Penguin Group Ireland, 25 St. Stephen's Green, Dublin 2, Ireland (a division of Penguin Books Ltd.)
Penguin Group (Australia), 250 Camberwell Road, Camberwell, Victoria 3124, Australia
(a division of Pearson Australia Group Pty. Ltd.)
Penguin Books India Pvt. Ltd., 11 Community Centre, Panchsheel Park, New Delhi—110 017,
India
Penguin Group (NZ), cnr. Airborne and Rosedale Roads, Albany, Auckland 1310, New Zealand
(a division of Pearson New Zealand Ltd.)
Penguin Books (South Africa) (Pty.) Ltd., 24 Sturdee Avenue, Rosebank, Johannesburg 2196,
South Africa
Penguin Books Ltd., Registered Offices: 80 Strand, London WC2R 0RL, England

Copyright © 2005 by Natavi Guides, Inc.
Text design by Tiffany Estreicher.
Cover design and art by Liz Sheehan.

PRINTING HISTORY
Prentice Hall Press trade paperback edition / August 2005

The Prentice Hall Press logo is a trademark belonging to Penguin Group (USA) Inc.

This book has been cataloged by the Library of Congress

PRINTED IN THE UNITED STATES OF AMERICA

10   9   8   7   6   5   4   3   2   1

No doubt you've been bombarded with "expert" advice from your parents, professors, and countless advisors. It's time you got advice you can really use—from fellow students who've been where you're headed.

All Students Helping Students® books are written and edited by top students and recent grads from colleges and universities across the United States. You'll find no preachy or condescending advice here—just stuff to help you succeed in tackling your academic, social, and professional challenges.

To learn more about Students Helping Students® books, read samples and student-written articles, share your own experiences with other students, suggest a topic, or ask questions, visit us at www. StudentsHelpingStudents.com!

We're always looking for fresh minds and new ideas!

A Note from the Founders of Students Helping Students®

Dear Reader,

Welcome to Students Helping Students®!

Before you dive headfirst into reading this book, we wanted to take a moment to share with you where Students Helping Students® came from and where we're headed.

It was only a few years ago that we graduated from college, having made enough mistakes to fill a *War and Peace*–sized novel, learned more and different things than we expected going in, and made some tough decisions—often without having enough advice to help us out. As we thought about our college experiences, we realized that some of the best and most practical advice we ever got came from our classmates and recent grads. And that's how the idea for Students Helping Students® books was born.

Our vision for Students Helping Students® is simple: Allow high school and college students to learn from fellow students who can share brutally honest and practical advice based on their own experiences. We've designed our books to be brief and to the point—we've been there and know that students don't have a minute to waste. They are extremely practical, easy to read, and inexpensive, so they don't empty your wallet.

As with all firsts, we're bound to do some things wrong, and if you have reactions or ideas to share with us, we can't wait to hear them. Visit www.StudentsHelpingStudents.com to submit your comments online.

Thanks for giving us a shot!

—Nataly and Avi
Creators of Students Helping Students®

Student Editors

Julio Machado studied history and literature at Harvard University. He has written other guides for college students, including several literature study guides and a handbook for writing the perfect application essay. As of this guide's publication date, he's still working on his first great novel, which should be completed within the next fifty to sixty years.

Mike Yank recently graduated from Harvard University with a degree in History and Science. When he first entered college, Mike had a vague interest in comedy that later became sharpened and intensified as he pursued various extracurricular activities. As a member of his school's television organization, he had the opportunity to explore comedy by writing for a sketch show and for a sitcom, which inspired him to join the campus's humor magazine, *The Harvard Lampoon*. Mike soon realized that he could try to make a living out of his interest by attempting to break into the entertainment industry, and a few months after graduating, he moved to Hollywood and began writing spec scripts.

After a few months, he found his current job as a writer for

Animax Interactive, a company that develops animated comedies. He plans to continue to pursue a career in writing for television in the immediate future, and he hopes that some smart network executive will offer him a job within the next year.

Student Contributors

Students from Amherst College, Babson College, Bates College, Boston College, Boston University, Brown University, California State University–Long Beach, Carleton College, Castleton State College, Columbia University, Cornell University, Dartmouth College, Denison College, Emory University, Florida International University, Franklin and Marshall College, George Washington University, Georgetown University, Georgia Tech, Harvard University, Hunter College–CUNY, James Madison University, Middlebury College, Middle Tennessee State University, New York University, Northwestern University, Pratt Institute, Rutgers University, San Diego State University, Santa Clara University, Seton Hall University, Simon Fraser University, Stanford University, Trinity College, the University of California–Santa Barbara, the University of Colorado–Boulder, the University of Delaware, the University of Florida, the University of Kansas, the University of Massachusetts–Amherst, the University of North Carolina, the University of Pennsylvania, the University of Rhode Island, the University of Toronto, the University of Wisconsin–Madison, the University of Wisconsin–Oshkosh, the University of Wisconsin–Whitewater, Wellesley College, Wesleyan University, the College of William and Mary, and Yale University contributed to this guide.

Julio's Note

We've tried to collect a lot of useful advice in this guide, and some of it will undoubtedly sound familiar to you. Figuring out what you should major in isn't rocket science, and we can't claim to give you a secret tip no one else has thought of before. But if you pay some attention to the advice that dozens of students have shared in this guide, you might think of a thing or two that helps you find a major that genuinely interests you and makes your college experience a great one.

Mike's Note

Somewhere along the several years you spent in college, you're supposed to figure out what exactly it is you want to do when you graduate, or at least what you're interested in. Some people get to college already knowing they want to be doctors or lawyers, while others find that their vague interest in English as high school students blossoms into a passion that drives them to apply to graduate school so they can become professors.

I decided that I wanted to try to become a comedy writer, but unfortunately, my college didn't have a comedy-writing major. Fortunately, we did have a humor magazine, to which I duly devoted myself. The magazine and other similar extracurriculars with which I was involved became the core of my college experience. It's my hope that this guide inspires you to take advantage of the open, "anything can happen" atmosphere of college and discover your true passion and interests—no matter how elusive they may seem.

Contents

FISHING FOR
A MAJOR

What It Is

For most of us, choosing a major is a somewhat daunting task. One day you're thinking marketing, the next day you take a philosophy class and suddenly, you've uncovered a new life passion. Your parents keep bugging you to do something practical with your college years and your life and to start doing it right away. And on top of this, you're so busy with classes, activities, and your work-study job that you hardly have any time to think about your major.

Here are our two cents on choosing a major: In many ways, it's a process of self-discovery. It's the search for what you're truly interested in, for what you feel you can happily study for the few years you spend in college. Don't worry too much at this point about whether someone will actually pay you money to do what you love or if your major will make your parents proud. If you're happy and learning about something you genuinely find interesting, you'll find a way to make it work.

Choosing a major can often be frustrating. There will be days when you simply refuse to think about your future as it rushes toward you like a locomotive. You'll want to tear your student handbook to pieces as you wonder again and again, *"Why* do I have to choose a major?" Totally normal, and yes, most of us have been there. The key is to start early, explore as much as possible, and listen to your gut.

Like many other big decisions, choosing a major is usually as fruitful a process as you're willing to make it. If you're honest with yourself—if you finally admit that you hate chemistry and would much rather spend your time reading about American history, for example—then your chances of having a great college experience will be pretty high. If you shy away from facing reality, or just simply don't put too much thought into finding a major that makes you happy, you'll run the risk of making yourself miserable. We definitely vote for the former.

What It's Not

Choosing a major is not a curse thrown upon you by evil academic forces. The process definitely can be frustrating—too little advising, too much pressure to choose right away, too many choices, too little time to figure it all out. Keep in mind that choosing a major is an important part of your college experience and one that's worth carefully thinking about. The world is much too vast to tackle all at once. You have to stake your claim on a little piece of it and build a home.

Choosing a major is not irrelevant or unimportant. Your field of study will speak to you constantly—through advisors, professors, course requirements, and fellow students. Whatever choices you make after college, your major will continue to matter through the years. It will affect you, enrich your mind, expand your options, and for some, define the course of your life. Make an effort to find the right major, and you might get more out of college than you ever expected.

At the same time, your major is not necessarily something that will monumentally and irreversibly affect the rest of your life. There are so many great things to learn about that you could spend your college years studying something very interesting without it actually relating in any way to your future career. On the flip side, if you absolutely despise what you study in college, it doesn't mean that you'll be miserably stuck with it for the rest of your life.

1

Getting to Know Yourself

There are many ways to choose a major: random selection, choosing the first thing that comes to mind, pin-the-tail-on-the-major, following your parents' advice, and so on. But if your goal is to make your college years as productive and rewarding as possible (and hey, we think that's a worthy goal), you should seriously consider a more organized and thoughtful approach. We hate to use a cliché, but here goes: To find a major that makes you happy, you need to get to know yourself. The greatest service you can do yourself and your potential major is to seek out your interests and then figure out how to match them to a major.

Keep in mind that you don't have to know what you want to do with the rest of your life—or even what you want to do after college—to choose a great major that interests you.

College is the ideal place to explore new ideas, disciplines, and interests as long as you give yourself the time and freedom to do it. You'll probably feel an immense pressure to choose a career path and stick to it, but you have to be strong and resist it for at least a short while. Even if you're pretty sure that you know where you're headed, it can't hurt to take a look around.

C'mon, what do you have to lose?

- I Want to Know More About . . .
- College Goals
- The Usual Suspects
- Unfamiliar Territory

I Want to Know More About . . .

Don't do what you think will get you a lot of money or what other people tell you to do, but do what you really enjoy.

—Junior
Harvard University

It seems like too many of us enter college with a particular career in mind and we choose our majors accordingly. Your parents might be pretty happy if you choose the security and financial rewards of a pre-med or business track, for example, but if that's not what you find interesting or rewarding, you'll be dooming yourself to four years of misery—or many more. A better idea is to put your thoughts of a career on hold for a while and open your mind to every possibility before narrowing down your choices of a major.

Start your search for a major by thinking about the things you enjoy doing—reading thick history books, writing short stories, coming up with new business ideas, hanging out with your friends, and solving their life problems—and try to include some academic things as well. If you're having a hard time thinking of real interests, then you may need to take some time and get to know yourself. Think about your high school and junior high experiences. When did you feel most comfortable or most excited about what you were doing? What were your favorite classes? Was there ever a moment when you thought, "I think I'd enjoy doing this for the rest of my life." Grab those moments and remember them as you begin to consider potential fields of study.

You might find it helpful to make a list of your interests to keep in the back of your pocket as you begin to search for a major. This list will be a great reminder that whatever major you choose shouldn't be something you feel you have to do but rather something you want to study for the next few years of your life.

Finally, keep in mind that there may be academic fields that you've never encountered or considered that could keep you interested and happy as you study them for the next several years. If you're the kind of person who enjoys being challenged, then your college years will allow you to explore vast tracts of uncharted territory, and you may discover a few surprises along the way. Leave a few blank spaces at the end of every list you make for the strengths and interests that you never knew you had.

Self-Inquisition

This getting to know yourself might sound like a hokey thing to do, but trust us, it helps. You don't want to end up with a major and potential career path that you don't end up enjoying so give it a shot. Here are some questions to consider:

✓ What were some of your favorite classes in high school? Why?

✓ What classes do you wish you had taken but didn't for whatever reason?

✓ What do you like to spend most of your time doing outside of the classroom?

✓ What is one thing you've always been interested in academically and have not yet pursued?

✓ What is one skill you've always wanted to learn? An instrument? Computer programming?

College Goals

I've always thought I'd be the starving-artist type, but then I ran into some money problems sophomore year and I had to eat ramen noodles for three weeks. I still want to be an artist, but I want to be well fed.

—Sophomore
Cornell University

So, what do you want to get out of your major? This might seem like a silly question, but seriously, give it some thought. Some of us choose a certain field of study because we're curious about it and want to spend the next few years learning about it in as much depth as possible. Others look for a major that teaches them some practical skills they can apply in their future career. And of course, there are those of us who don't really know what we want out of our major and choose it at the very last minute because that's what our advisor is telling us we have to do.

As you begin to think about your choice, give some thought to what you want to get out of your major and college in general. There's no right answer—at least not one we've figured out—but there is an answer that makes sense to you. Think about it and try to be as brutally honest as possible. You might be dead-set on what you want to do after graduation and to major in something that prepares you for it. Or you might have absolutely no idea what you want to have for breakfast, never mind four years from now, and look for a major that interests you but that doesn't necessarily have a clear career choice attached to it. Don't be intimidated by the idea of

 ## Julio's Corner

When I first started college, I was thinking about studying computer science as a way to earn a big salary and support my writing career. I thought I might develop some brilliant new method for generating artificial intelligence as I worked on a groundbreaking novel in my plentiful leisure time. I later realized that four years was a long time to study something I only half-liked, and I began looking for a better option.

thinking about such grand things as your life goals—you're much more likely to pick a major that makes you happy if you do.

You should always keep in mind, however, that your goals can and will change. The more you learn, the more rewarding your career decisions will be. Keep your options open at all times. Take a wide variety of courses and pursue every possible interest. Let the four years you spend in college affect your career—and life—aspirations. The world will be very different by the time you graduate, and you'll have to be prepared to deal with that new reality.

The Usual Suspects

I took a few classes, but mostly I looked at all the concentrations and asked, which one of these interests me the most, and that's where I started researching. I also looked at the requirements for some of them, which courses I had to take and how many.

—Junior
Harvard University

Based on your interests and your goals you can probably come up with five to seven likely suspects for your major. Something we found works really well is taking some time to read through your college's course catalogue, paying particular attention to subjects that match your interests. Here are a few things to consider:

✓ What classes are offered as part of each major you're considering and do they sound interesting to you?

(Remember to look at both the intro and the more advanced courses.)

✓ What type of classes will you have to take: large lectures or small seminars?

✓ What type of work will you be doing: reading tons of long, dense books; writing many papers; taking tests; or conducting experiments?

The idea here is to not only match the subject matter of your major with your interests but to also make sure that you'll enjoy doing the type of work that your classes will involve. (Yes, we just used "enjoy" when talking about classwork because even if we hate to admit it, there is such a thing!)

As you come up with a few majors that seem like they might be for you, write them down. Having a list of your usual suspects will be really helpful as you do more research to figure out which one will be your home for the next several years.

Unfamiliar Territory

If I had to choose now, I probably would've studied economics. I hated economics at the time I was choosing my major, but I didn't really know a whole lot about it.

—Junior
Harvard University

As you look through your list of probable majors, keep in mind that there are many, many fields that you've never really had time to explore. Where else are you going to get that chance if not in college? You may think you understand every field out there but you won't know unless you make the effort to venture into unfamiliar territory and explore all of your options. At worst, you'll spend a few credits; at best, you'll discover a potentially life-altering new passion.

Take some time to venture into parts of the course catalogue that you might not know much about. Pay particular attention to fields that you didn't have the chance to explore in high school. Colleges tend to offer much broader variety than most high schools, and you may have never had the opportunity to study things like Sanskrit or neurobiology until now.

Also check out some disciplines that you've always thought were definitely not for you. Are you an artist at heart? Peruse the computer science or economics section for more than ten seconds, if you can take it. Are you a hardcore statistics buff? Check out history or philosophy courses. You might surprise yourself.

 Julio's Corner

Freshman year, I was like a chipmunk on speed. I woke up every morning with the kind of energy the gods must have, and it never seemed to run out. If you've just started college, you might still be feeling this kind of excitement. My advice to you is to take advantage of it while it lasts: Plan ahead, make schedules, and set goals. In a few months, when the high has begun to wear off, you'll still have these plans to follow and you'll be incredibly thankful.

As you explore new fields of study, keep track of what appeals to you. A newly found interest might not turn into a major, but you might choose it as a minor, or it might turn into a special project within your major. In the chapters that follow, we'll discuss a process through which you can research, understand, and nail down your ideal major. As you go through it, be sure to keep with you your list of "never-thought-I'd-like-this-but-I-might majors." If your college experience is at all typical, you'll probably end up choosing something you never expected.

We Talk With . . .

Jacob, Junior, Brown University

What advice would you offer to other college students about choosing a major?
The best thing about my major (sociology) is that it has allowed me plenty of freedom to take electives. I love sociology and I'm happy with my decision, but there's no way I would enjoy taking classes only in that or any other major. Many of the electives I have taken have done more to define my college experience that classes in my major. That's one of the reasons deciding on a major early in your college career is a good idea. I know people who spent three years switching back and forth between majors, only to find themselves struggling to meet the required class minimum in their major senior year. Choosing a major might seem like a huge decision with long-term consequences, but my advice is to settle in early on a major you like and just go with it. If you can do this, you'll allow yourself more time to experience what really makes college great.

2

Thinking About Your Career

As you begin to think about your major, more likely than not thoughts and questions about what you'll do with your life after college will creep into your mind. Will a degree in music theory help you feed yourself and later your family? Do you need to major in economics to become an entrepreneur? Can you major in philosophy and still go on to medical school and become a doctor?

It's a good idea to give your potential career some thought, but what we don't recommend is that you obsess about and choose a major that you think will lead to it. You should choose a major that lets you study things you really enjoy. If you enjoy them, there is at least a chance that you will want to have a post-college job that has something to do with them.

Also keep in mind that what you do outside of class—during an internship or as an extracurricular activity—can have as much, if not more, impact on your future career as your major. Just because you major in English doesn't mean that you'll like journalism; but if you love writing for your school paper, it might mean that a journalist is deep within you.

- Major Doesn't Mean Career
- What Do You Want to Be When You Grow Up?
- Informational Interview 101
- Know Your Requirements
- Taste of the Real World

Major Doesn't Mean Career

Don't think that because you want to go into business that you have to study business. If you want to be an artist, you don't necessarily have to study art. When I look at a résumé, I don't look for a particular degree. I ask myself, what can this person bring to the job that no one else can? I can teach you to use business software; I can't duplicate the kind of growth you get from four years of college.

—Branch Manager, Ford Motors, Inc.
Music Major
Alabama State University '71

Unless you go to a vocational college—in which case you're clearly there to learn specific skills for a certain career—you shouldn't think of your major as a way to prepare for a certain job after you graduate. Or even as a way to find out what type of job you'd like to have. Just because you take and love every psychology class offered in the curriculum doesn't mean

We Talk With . . .

Siobhan, Copy Editor
Recent Grad, Columbia University

What was your major in college?
I majored in English with a minor in writing.

Why did you choose it as your major?
My main interest was writing. I knew I wanted to take creative writing classes when I got to school and I thought it would be a good idea to major in something that would enhance my writing. I had always been interested in literature, so it seemed like a natural choice.

Were you happy with your choice?
I was very happy. I couldn't have imagined majoring in anything else.

What did you end up doing after graduation?
My main love is playwriting. I made lots of playwright friends at school. It's really great, because we're all still in touch and have a writing group that meets every three weeks. I feel really fortunate. It's so important to have support—people to read your work and offer useful feedback—if you're trying to do anything creative. I earn my living as a copy editor and writer, and my major helped get that work, too.

Did your major help you or hurt you in your search for a job?
It definitely helped. Most of the people I've met through work have majors in either English or communications.

Did your major give you the skills to succeed at your first job?
I didn't need to have knowledge of literature to do my first job as a copy editor at a trade magazine. Basically, I needed writing and editing skills, which I learned at school through writing papers.

---

that you'll love being a psychologist. And not doing well in your econ class doesn't mean that your dream to become an entrepreneur is any less real. In fact, many people working in business today don't have business or economics degrees. Music and history majors often end up as branch managers or entrepreneurs, and they thrive in their positions.

Try not to worry about knowing what you want to do after college, at least for a few years. You'll have all the time in the world—including the last few years of college—to think about and figure out what your post-college job might be. But you won't have another opportunity like this to really explore different academic fields, learn the different skills that they offer, and train your mind to think about things as different as art history and statistics. An English class won't completely prepare you for a career in publishing, but it will teach you how to write well, and that's a skill that you definitely want to acquire.

If you choose a major that truly interests you and pushes you to learn, you'll gain a great set of skills that you can then use in any career. It sounds so idealistic, but it's true. Employers don't expect you to start your first job knowing exactly how to do it—on-the-job training is a core learning component that almost all careers offer. But employers do expect you to be a well-rounded person, have solid writing and communication skills, and the ability and training to learn new things and excel at them.

RECENT GRADS LOOK BACK

We Talk With . . .

Nataly, Cofounder of Students Helping
Students®, Recent Grad,
Wesleyan University

What was your major in college?
A funky program called the College of Social Studies. Basically,
political science combined with economics, with some philosophy and history thrown in just for fun.

Why did you choose it as your major?
I liked that there would only be thirty or so people from each
class selected for this program—I do much better in smaller
groups, and that was important. The biggest class had fifteen
people, another plus for me. Another reason was my vague
thoughts—and my parents' clearer thoughts—about potentially
going to law school after college, and this major covered the
right disciplines. I did want to study econ, but not in a quantita-
tive sort of way, so this offered a method to do that. And I'd
heard through the rumor mill that some great profs taught
courses in the major, which was a huge plus.

Were you happy with your choice?
For the most part, I'd have to say yes. I liked the subject matter,
the professors, and the small tutorials. It was really intense and
made me feel a bit isolated from the rest of the Wesleyan
crowd, but I tried to manage that by taking outside classes.

What did you end up doing after graduation?
I went to work for McKinsey & Co., the consulting megahouse,
in New York. I'd interned with them one summer, and although I
never thought of being a consultant, the job seemed interesting

and everyone and their brother wanted to work there, so I figured I should give it a shot.

Did your major help you or hurt you in your search for a job?
To be honest, I don't think it made much of a difference. I know McKinsey was looking for people with diverse backgrounds, and I filled the "general political science" niche. But they also hired art majors, physics majors, and all sorts of other funky majors.

Did your major give you the skills to succeed at your first job?
Yes, but not through the subject matter that I learned. I mean, I learned economics, but it was so theoretical that I could not really apply it to my job in any way. But my major required that we write a ridiculous amount of papers and I found that my writing skills were pretty strong and important in my job as an analyst. So much of what happens at any job I think is communication—written and verbal—and those are the skills that I brought from college, and from my major.

What Do You Want to Be When You Grow Up?

Your college major doesn't have to be related in any way to what you do after you graduate. True. But thinking about what career you might want to pursue can help you in your major search. The career services office at your school is a great resource to help you sort out your ideas about what major you might choose and how it might relate to the few career choices you're contemplating. Check it out and if you can, definitely spend some time with a career counselor. Although

We Talk With . . .

Rachel, English Teacher, Recent Grad,
University of Pennsylvania

What was your major in college?
I was an English major with a concentration in twentieth-century African-American literature.

Why did you choose it as your major?
I chose it because writing was a strength for me, as well as something I enjoyed. I couldn't imagine majoring in something that didn't interest me for the sake of a career that didn't even exist yet. I concentrated in the area of literature that I liked most.

Were you happy with your choice?
I was definitely happy with my choice. English provides you with a good foundation no matter what your future profession may be. Even corporate America is recruiting English majors because they need their analytical and writing skills.

What did you end up doing after graduation?
I'm a novelist and a high school English teacher.

Did your major help you or hurt you in your search for a job?
Of course, being an English teacher, my major was essential for my job. But I still feel that if I ever decided to change careers dramatically, that English was the right decision for an undergrad major. Sometimes making your major too specific (European international relations, for example) can hinder the job search.

Did your major give you the skills to succeed at your first job? Not really. You need to know books to be a good English teacher, but you need to know how to control a classroom more. That's something that can't really be taught in college. This is true for most jobs. The skills you need on the job are really not what you learn in school, so you might as well just study what you want and figure everything else out later.

---

you might feel that career counselors are reserved for those actively looking for a job, they aren't. They're there to talk to all students and can be extremely helpful. Go ahead and set up an appointment and you might be surprised at the advice you receive.

Talk to a career counselor about your interests and your goals, including what you think you might want to do with your life after graduation. Try not to focus so much on a particular career at this point, but rather, on things that you would like to be doing—painting, teaching, traveling, researching, interacting with people, building skyscrapers, and so on. Career counselors probably interact with more students and alumni than most other advisors on campus, and they learn quite a bit about the paths that students take and the majors that lead them there.

If a particular college major is critical for your desired career, then visiting the career services office is not an option, but a requirement. Here you'll find detailed job descriptions, alumni databases, and a dozen other useful sources. Make sure to also check graduate school information and related requirements.

Julio's Corner

Don't dismiss career aptitude tests entirely. The questions on those things tend to be loaded ("Do you like to work with heavy machinery?"), so that you're always second-guessing the test. If you do your best to avoid doing this, though, you can get a pretty good reading on your skills. I took an aptitude test in elementary school and it told me I was going to be a writer. Go figure.

And don't miss out on taking a career aptitude test, if you can find one. While you might think you know exactly what you want to do, it never hurts to explore your options.

RECENT GRADS LOOK BACK

We Talk With . . .

Lee, Television Writer, Recent Grad, Connecticut College

What was your major in college?
English, with a concentration in creative writing.

Why did you choose it as your major?
I've always been interested in a writer's motivation—why a writer writes what he writes. As a fledgling writer myself, I figured what better way to improve my own work than to closely examine the works of others?

Were you happy with your choice?
I feel that starting to write as much as I did in college—both creatively and analytically—made me much more comfortable after graduation to sit in a room by myself and "create."

What did you end up doing after graduation?
I moved out to L.A. to pursue a career as a television and feature film writer.

Did your major help you or hurt you in your search for a job?
I think it helped me. It showed an aptitude for reading and writing, perhaps the two most underrated skills in the workforce.

Did your major give you the skills to succeed at your first job?
Well, my first job was as an administrative assistant, so I'm fairly convinced that a well-trained chimp could have handled those duties. As I progressed beyond those initial menial tasks, I feel that my ability to write clearly and quickly set me apart from my contemporaries.

Informational Interview 101

I've wanted to be a doctor since I was four, so when I got to college, I was pretty much set on majoring in biology, or organic chemistry, or something like that. After talking to a few medical school students, though, I discovered that the best majors are the unexpected ones. That's how I ended up in the psychology department.

—Senior
Amherst College

We Talk With . . .

Jason, Recent Grad,
George Washington University

What was your major in college?
Journalism.

Why did you choose it as your major?
I had thought of an English major but decided against it. I wanted a major that would allow me to write, but the style of writing I was using in my English classes was not fulfilling to me. A friend was a journalism major and I decided to look into it.

Were you happy with your choice?
Very. I was able to write in a style of my choice. Although my reporting classes had a more strict style, most classes allowed me to use a bit of creative writing in my pieces. I was lucky to have excellent professors that allowed me to experiment with style. The classes didn't feel like sitting in a classroom. Discussions would take place on current events and there were few textbooks. The piece of text most used in these classes was that day's copy of the *Washington Post* (I went to school in Washington, DC).

What did you end up doing after graduation?
My first job was with a small video production company in DC.

Did your major help you or hurt you in your search for a job?
It helped very much, although it may seem odd that it did. I am now working in television, as opposed to print media (which was my focus in college). Employers are always looking for people that have the skills to write and express themselves clearly.

Did your major give you the skills to succeed at your first job? The skills I learned in journalism helped me excel at my first job and have continued to help me in my career. Journalism gives one a keen eye of analysis. It teaches you to organize thoughts and plan actions. While I did not become a reporter for a newspaper I still use the skills I learned in my journalism classes.

Your potential future career and your college major may not and don't need to have much in common. But if you do have some career ideas in mind and you'd like to know what kinds of classes and fields you might find useful, consider seeking out some recent grads and alumni and talking to them. Do you need to study art history to manage an art gallery? Does a math major mean that you'll have a hard time getting a job in the music industry? Recent grads are still fresh on their college experience and have tasted a bit of the real career world—they can offer some useful ideas and are pretty easy to find.

You might know some recent grads in your family, among your friends, or people you've worked with. Give them a call, see how they are, and tell them about your quest for a major. If there's one thing we've learned in writing this guide it's that people love to talk about themselves. Don't worry about imposing on their time—who doesn't like to be asked for their sage advice?

If you don't personally know any recent grads or your college alumni, check out the alumni database at the career center. You'll probably be able to search it by location, year of graduation, major, and career field. Use it to find a few recent grads who are doing what you might like to be doing in a few years. Send them an email to introduce yourself and ask if you could briefly speak to them about their jobs and their postcollege experiences. Just make it very clear that what you're looking for is advice and not a job.

Many alumni are overloaded with requests for jobs or internships that are disguised as requests for advice, and most don't like any of these sneaky maneuvers. Avoid bad first impressions by clearly stating that you're in the process of searching for a major and would like some advice. Pay some compliments—it will get you everywhere. For example: "I think your job as a (fill in the blank) sounds wonderful and I'd like to find out how your college experience helped you get to this point."

If you get a positive response, arrange to talk by phone, if possible. Jot down some *specific* questions to give the conversation some structure because phone silence is *really* uncomfortable. Here are some examples of what you might want to ask:

✓ What was your major and how did you end up choosing it?
✓ Could you tell me about what you did after college and how you got to your current job?
✓ Do you think that your major helped you succeed in getting a job after college? Do you think it helps you do your current job better?
✓ Do you think that I should major in (fill in the blank) to be able to get a job in your field?
✓ What are some important skills I should aim to get in order to succeed in your career?

✓ Do you think it really matters what I major in with re-spect to being able to get a job in your industry?

And make sure to thank whomever you talk to—besides being polite, you want to leave a good impression in case you do need to discuss job opportunities in the future.

RECENT GRADS LOOK BACK

We Talk With . . .

Kate, Graduate Student in Psychology, Recent Grad, Wellesley College

What was your major in college?
Psychology.

Why did you choose it as your major?
I wanted to work with people to help relieve suffering.

Were you happy with your choice?
Yes.

What did you end up doing after graduation?
Two years as a research assistant in a psychiatry department and then a doctoral program in clinical psychology.

Did your major help you or hurt you in your search for a job?
It helped me, but my research experience, which was not re-quired for my major, was the most helpful.

Did your major give you the skills to succeed at your first job?
Sort of. Organizational skills helped me the most.

Know Your Requirements

We Talk With . . .

Avi, Cofounder of Students Helping Students®, Recent Grad, Wesleyan University

What was your major in college?
English, plain and simple.

Why did you choose it as your major?
I've always loved to read and write and discuss readings and writings. As an English major, that's pretty much what you do most of the time, so it worked out very well.

Were you happy with your choice?
I was happy with my choice, as I was able to spend most of my academic time doing what I really liked to do, but I do regret not having taken a wider variety of courses, like econ or philosophy.

What did you end up doing after graduation?
I worked for a medium-size book publishing company, Henry Holt.

Did your major help you or hurt you in your search for a job?
The mere fact that I was an English major helped get me the job, but the job itself turned out to be educational yet horribly boring. Into my second and third jobs, my writing, analytical, and communication skills—which I like to think were honed as an English major—proved to be very useful.

Did your major give you the skills to succeed at your first job? Yes, in the writing that I had to do, but nothing can prepare you for the inevitable office gofering that happens with an entry-level job in publishing (not to mention the meager salaries).

The best candidates are well balanced. We get so many biology and physiology majors applying here, it's refreshing to see someone who studied environmental science or computer engineering.

—Admissions Officer, UCLA School of Medicine
Physical Sciences Major
University of California–Berkeley '82

For those of you who hope to become doctors, lawyers, or career academics, the courses you take now will be an important part of your overall career development. You should make sure that you know if there are any specific course requirements and allow time in your four-year schedule to get them done.

If you're planning to go on to medical school, for example, you have no choice but to fulfill the required courses, like the often-dreaded organic chemistry. Your choice of major, however, offers surprising flexibility. Don't get locked into the obvious choices right away—biology, political science, etc. There are many ways to meet your pre-med or pre-law requirements, and you should seriously consider selecting an unrelated primary major and meeting those requirements on the side.

RECENT GRADS LOOK BACK

We Talk With . . .

Gabe, Graduate Student in History, Recent Grad, Wesleyan University

What was your major in college?
History.

Why did you choose it as your major?
I ultimately chose it based on the quality of the professors and the love of a particular subject they instilled in me. I think as you're thinking about your major you have to ask yourself many, many questions, such as: What types of problems will I confront? What types of books will I have to read? What type of reasoning do I feel most comfortable with?

If you're considering an academic path, you'll find it hard to get into history graduate school if you studied art and vice versa. In fact, you may find it hard to get into history graduate school for eighteenth-century European political history if you've studied, say, twentieth-century social history in America.

Were you happy with your choice?
Yes, it opened up a whole world.

What did you end up doing after graduation?
I ended up working in city government and found that the writing and research skills were quite relevant and useful.

Did your major help you or hurt you in your search for a job?
I think my major was irrelevant.

Did your major give you the skills to succeed at your first job?
Yes, I talked on the phone a lot and history gives you lots to say.

Taste of the Real World

We Talk With . . .

Ben, Recent Grad, Haverford College

What was your major in college?
Economics.

Why did you choose it as your major?
Econ is more about learning an approach to decision making and problem solving than it is about memorizing how the GDP is different from the GNP. Fundamentally, it provides a model based on the core concepts of supply, demand, opportunity cost, risk, etc. in which it is possible to make an empirical judgment as to what course of action is the best. I always found the economists' mind-set to be an interesting and useful one when trying to make decisions in my own life, and economics has become an inextricable part of the way I think.

Were you happy with your choice?
Yup.

What did you end up doing after graduation?
I worked in I-banking for a few years in New York. I learned a lot and got to do very interesting work, but the hours are murder (80 on a good week, 100+ when things got busy).

Did your major help you or hurt you in your search for a job?
It helped me a lot. Employers seem to sense that economics provides the tools for making informed, sensible decisions, even in the face of incomplete or overwhelming information.

Did your major give you the skills to succeed at your first job?
Yes. I can't imagine a job that would not make use of the
things economics teaches. Even a gardener could benefit
from such concepts as expected value and opportunity cost
when deciding which fertilizer to buy, or how to spend their
time if they have too many tasks to do in a limited amount of
time.

One of the best ways to learn about different jobs and careers is through internships. By diving headfirst into a career
field you get much more than any guidebook or dozens of informational interviews can ever provide: a real taste of what
it might be like to actually work in that particular area after
graduation. For example, you may think that you really want
to become an editor at a publishing house but after giving it a
trial run through a summer internship decide that you'd
rather pursue a more fast-paced career as a newspaper editor.
Figuring out what you don't want to do as a career is sometimes as valuable as finding your true calling, and internships
can allow you to do both.

Start your search for internships early in the year—the
best ones go fast. Check out listings at the career services offices and online internship websites like www.internshippro-
grams.com. Try to keep an open mind and take a summer or
two to venture into a career field that interests you but you
don't know much about. The great thing about internships is
that they are a trial run: You get to do them for a few
months, without having to commit to a serious job for several years.

My Writing Internship

by Ellen, Senior, Columbia University

I loved creative writing when I was little, but as I got older and school became more time-consuming, I stopped writing for myself and started writing for school. It wasn't until I got to college that I had the opportunity to reignite my passion for writing in the form of a creative-writing class. As much as I loved to write, though, I still worried about what would happen when I entered the "real" world. I certainly couldn't count on writing to pay for rent, food, clothing, and whatever else I might need.

It wasn't until the summer before my senior year that I found an internship at Simon & Schuster that satisfied both my love of writing and my need to make a living. If I entered the publishing industry, I realized, I'd have a full-time job *and* I'd learn how to become a published writer. My fantasy of becoming a writer always involved something like me sending my manuscript off to a big-name publisher, where they would be so astounded by my brilliance that they would offer me a three-book deal on the spot. Obviously, I had no concept of how much work it takes to get a book published, but interning in one of Simon & Schuster's editorial departments provided the behind-the-scenes experience I needed to snap me out of my fantasy world. It was a bit depressing to see how many manuscripts were rejected each week, but by reading all of those submissions I learned the difference between a good book proposal and a mediocre one. I learned what I would need to do when I submitted *my* manuscript so that it wouldn't get lost in the slush pile.

In addition to the on-the-job experience, one of the editors took me under her wing and talked to me about my writing "career." Even in my fantasies I'd never used the word "career" when I thought about writing. To hear an editor use that word—in reference to *me*!—boosted my confidence more than anything else could have. I'm still not sure whether I intend to make a "career" out of writing, but at least now I'm not afraid to try.

3

Exploring Your Major Options

Ultimately, the only way to really get to know what a certain major might be like is to take a few courses in that department. It's not enough that you took similar classes in high school, or that you've read some related books (unless, of course, you've read *all* the books). You won't know for sure what interests you and what doesn't until you've done some real coursework, and you won't do any coursework unless you take some courses.

You won't always have the luxury of choice—your college will probably require that you take some classes that you'd never otherwise consider—but even within the tightest requirements, you'll still have a little room to maneuver. Find a few courses that truly interest you and try to fit them into your schedule.

And as you go about selecting your classes, be gutsy and

venture into some unknown areas, as well as those that you think you might major in. You never know what new academic discipline will suddenly become your true passion.

- Try It on for Size
- Office Hours
- These Mouths Don't Lie
- Surprise Yourself
- Core Curriculum Adventures
- Make It Count
- Good Advice is Priceless

Try It on for Size

The first classes I looked at were business classes. I'd always wanted to study business, so that's where I started when I had to register.

Senior
University of Colorado–Boulder

Remember that list of your probable majors? Use it as you look through your course catalogue to select a few classes. If you're a freshman or sophomore, your options will be somewhat limited by particular course requirements. Don't let this bother you too much. You can learn a lot from these intro classes, and the broader knowledge will probably come in handy later.

If you can manage it, go beyond the standard introductory courses—be courageous and take a few that are more advanced. Course material inevitably becomes more specific and demanding as you delve deeper into your field, and harder classes will give you a chance to test your ability to handle more complex subject matter. They'll also help you decide if this is the type of material that you want to learn about in tremendous depth over the course of a few years. For example, you might find that computer science is too theory-intensive

We Talk With . . .

Patricia, Senior,
Middlebury College

What is your major? Are you happy with it?
I'm a neuroscience major. And yeah, I'm happy with it. I didn't even realize I was going to be a neuroscience major, but the thing is, once we had to decide on our major sophomore year, I looked back and saw that most of the classes I had taken were in the neuroscience major. It was a natural progression. I thought I might want to do psychology, but I knew there wouldn't be as many options after graduation with that. Plus neuroscience was a smaller department.

What was most helpful in your process of deciding on your major?
I decided independently really, but talking to other neuroscience majors definitely helped.

What advice would you offer to other college students about choosing a major?
Don't be afraid to experiment. College is all about experimenting academically. Don't let your parents force you or your future. Even if you want to be a doctor or a lawyer, you don't have to be a certain major.

for your tastes or that art history relies too heavily on classification and codification to suit your style.

Office Hours

You can choose whatever major you like, but unless its core classes are taught by intriguing and knowledgeable professors who care about their students, you won't get nearly as much as you should out of it.

You've probably heard a few seniors or recent grads say that it was a few special professors who made their college education a great investment, and we think that's a great point to keep in mind. As you shop around for a major, you have to make sure that its faculty is as great as you'd like your professors and advisors to be. The quality of your professors can make or break your college experience.

Find out which professors teach courses in the fields you're interested in and go see them. Most hold office hours and some even devote a few office hours each month to speaking with prospective majors. Since current students frequent office hours to discuss assignments and class projects, you'll be a fresh and welcome change for the professor. Talk to him or her about the particular academic field, its core courses, and the professor's own academic interests. See if the professor is excited and engaged by what he or she is talking about, and whether this is someone you'd learn a lot from as a student.

You might not find that you like every professor you meet, but if you put in some effort and go to see a few of them in your potential majors, you'll have a much better idea of which field is best for you.

These Mouths Don't Lie

If it hadn't been for my roommates, I wouldn't have taken some of my favorite classes. If you're lucky enough to know a few people who share your outlook, you can learn from their mistakes and profit from their discoveries.

—Sophomore
University of California–Berkley

A great place to go for brutally honest advice about your potential major is your fellow classmates, particularly upperclassmen who've been through just about everything you're about to experience. They tend to be more approachable than professors or graduate students, and they're more likely to understand your particular concerns. Just remember that everyone has subjective tastes and biases, and you should take opinions and complaints with a grain of salt.

One of the best pieces of information your fellow students can share is the quality of different classes and professors. It's tough to judge what a class might be like from its description in the course catalogue, so ask students who've taken it. What material is covered? How interesting is it? How involved are the students in class discussion? Make sure to also get honest opinions about professors—their quality of teaching, how enthusiastic and accessible they are, and so on. Some schools even have websites where students rate professors and courses. If yours does, definitely check it out.

When asking fellow students about a particular class, remember that there are many reasons for disliking a course—and not all of them are easy to admit. Some students will complain about a professor's teaching style or the irrelevance of the readings, when in fact they attended only a few of the lectures and did only a fraction of the reading. You'll find that the slacker is a perennial source of misinformation, and that it's almost impossible to get a straight answer from the ultra-competitive crowd. Aim for students with similar interests and priorities to your own—they're more likely to give you useful information.

You'll also find it useful to talk to other students about the actual process of choosing a major. Where did they get the most helpful advice? Did auditing a few classes help or confuse them? What were some of the concerns that guided their decisions? Ask around, and try not to dismiss anything just because it seems strange or different.

We Talk With . . .

Laura, Junior, Santa Clara University

What is your major?
I'm a marketing major with a double minor in retail studies and international business.

Are you happy with it?
Yes, I am, definitely. I wanted to be a business major because I thought it would help with job opportunities after college, and marketing fit my personality traits the best—it definitely gave me a chance to use my strengths, like creativity.

What helped you decide on your major?

Talking to other students was most influential. Advisors don't do too much, and don't offer as much guidance as they do in high school. The problem is that they don't really know you or much about you. But professors can be helpful too—my first international business professor was so dynamic and interesting, so that definitely guided me.

What advice would you give to other students trying to choose a major?

Definitely talk to older students who you share other interests with. If you're similar to them personality or interest-wise, they can help guide you academically and help you figure out what you want to go into specifically. It helps to talk to students at your university, like business school for instance. But don't choose a major just because you think it's going to help you get a job after you graduate. It should be something that you're interested in, but will allow you more freedom to take other paths. I feel like many people choose majors based on job opportunities. For instance, my friend is a computer science major and is really bored, because she hates it and decided that as a major because she thought it would help her get a job. You'll just be unhappy for four years.

Surprise Yourself

Take the time to really read the course catalogue. Don't just look for stuff you think first-years should take.

—Sophomore
Wellesley College

Above all, take a chance. Enroll in a few classes that you might have never considered. Try some that seem intimidatingly different from the classes to which you're usually drawn. Allow that other side of your brain to get some nourishment and you might surprise yourself.

You have a unique opportunity in college to explore your intellect and your passions, so take advantage of it while you can. You might absolutely despise the class you take—and blame us for making you sit through hours of torture—but you'll save yourself a lot of "what-ifs" later on.

Try not to assume that just because you didn't do well in a particular discipline in high school, you can't be interested in it and ace it in college. High school classes can be pretty boring and not all teachers are inspiring. One great English prof in college can turn you on to Shakespeare in just a few weeks.

Besides, learning what you don't like is just as critical as finding out what genuinely interests you.

Core Curriculum Adventures

If I hadn't had to take a history core course, I'd be studying engineering right now. My parents are pissed, but I'm happy.

—Junior
Stanford University

In the last fifty years, many schools have adopted a core curriculum in order to give their students a well-rounded liberal education. The most common version consists of specialized introductory courses in several broad fields, such as literature, history, physical science, etc. Within this system, students are required to take at least a few courses in each of these fields before they graduate. For some, the core curriculum might be an irritating distraction in an already difficult and confusing environment. Other students like it because it helps them structure their course selection without too much stress. Whatever your view on this might be, chances are that your school will have some kind of a requirement system in place.

If you're stuck with requirements, you might as well take advantage of them. If you have to fulfill a history requirement, for example, choose an area of the world that interests you. For a literature requirement, consider taking a class that covers a book or an author that you like. There's bound to be a class or two within each discipline that interests you, so find it.

A core curriculum can be an important element in your quest to find a major. It forces you to take classes in a variety of disciplines, some of which you might have never otherwise considered. And if you'll pardon the cliché—you'll never know unless you try.

Liberal Arts

by Adele, Recent Grad,
New York University

When I entered college, I was terrified that I would be forced to choose a major right away. But my advisor encouraged me to shop around the different departments before making the big decision. This way, I not only made the choice that was best for me, but I was able to satisfy many of my core curriculum requirements during my freshman year. I also figured out that you could get to know the professors and other students in some departments by attending their lecture series and beginning-of-semester parties. A lot of programs have them and welcome students who haven't decided on a major yet. I ended up choosing an interdisciplinary major—comparative literature—where I not only studied great works of literature, but also took classes in history, philosophy, and foreign languages. I got to design my own program, where I took about half my classes in comparative literature and the other half in other humanities departments.

Even though I ended up falling in love with a very narrow field within my major, at first this multifaceted course of study appealed to me because it involved a lesser level of commitment to one department than say, the English literature or Spanish literature programs. A lot of my friends in the department were taking classes in sociology, psychology, anthropology, art history, linguistics—or anything else that appealed to them.

Make It Count

Signing up for classes in different departments that you're considering for your major is nice, but you won't learn much unless you put in some effort and do the work. Just about every student we talked to agrees on this much—you've gotta make it to class. Whatever else you do, going to class will keep you in touch with the course material and its particular approach to the subject. It will also keep you engaged and less bored than if you skip class and just do the work. Why go to college if you're not going to make it to class? You can read books and write papers on your own time; you have to go to *college* to attend classes.

Some large lectures can seem a little dull, but try to hang in there. You'll still learn something and get to know the subject matter better than if you just read books on your own. Plus you might meet some cool people and that's a nice bonus. Smaller classes are much more involved and you'll get a chance to interact with the professor and your fellow students; sometimes you learn more from your classmates than you do from any textbook. Smaller classes also mean that you have to know your stuff and come prepared, so you don't give a blank stare when it's your turn to contribute to the discussion.

We Talk With . . .

Rachel, Sophomore,
Franklin and Marshall College

What is your major?
I haven't declared yet because I want to try some new areas first before I decide.

What major are you thinking about?
I think I will choose creative writing because in spite of the endless amounts of reading and writing I have to do for all my classes, I still like to read fiction and write (yes, I even don't mind essays).

What is most helpful in your process of deciding on your major?
Knowing what I am interested in as well as being stubborn about it in terms of people who are doubtful about the practicality of

my potential major. I will be talking to my advisor and probably other students with similar interests more this fall.

What advice would you offer to other college students about choosing a major?
Find an area where you actually want to do the work, and stick with that instead of picking a major you hate and is boring. Do something where you will not end up grudging everything you do.

To really get a lot out of your classes you've got to put some effort into getting to know your professors. Make a little time and go to office hours. Ask your professors about their research, get their thoughts on their departments, and bring them questions about assignments and course materials. You'll find that you enjoy a course much more if you actually know the professor, and every lecture will seem more relevant and engaging. While many professors seem too busy to talk to students, they actually like and respect students who make a little extra effort. (And most love to talk about themselves and their work!)

If you fall behind on the reading in a certain class, our advice is not to try to catch up on all the material unless you think that you can do it quickly. Lagging behind the class will diminish your sense of belonging—you'll grow increasingly detached from the course and its progress, making it harder for you to understand what's going on. Do as much of each week's reading as you can and then move on, even if it means getting less from individual assignments.

Good Advice is Priceless

I was assigned an advisor right off the bat, but I didn't talk to her for months. I'm sorry I didn't go earlier, though. She was so helpful.

—Sophomore
Boston University

When you begin your freshman year, you'll probably be assigned an academic advisor. Depending on your school's advising policy, this person may be a professor, a dean, or a full-time counselor. In many cases, your advisor will not belong to the academic department that you're hoping to explore. This doesn't mean, however, that you can't get useful information from him or her. Rather, you should understand the limitations of your advisor's knowledge and seek outside help when necessary.

Although your advisor might not know everything about your particular fields of interest, he or she can be quite helpful in a general sense. You can discuss your ambitions, your concerns, and anything else that might be affecting your major-selection process. If nothing else, your assigned advisor can point you to the right places to go for more detailed and specific advice, and can be a good source of logistical information, such as when you must declare your major, what forms need to be filled out, etc.

Another resource that too few of us seem to take advantage of is departmental advising. There are usually two or three people within every department whose primary duties are to help prospective students within that major/field. These people will help you get to know the department before you join, which will give you plenty of time to avoid leaping into unfriendly waters. They can also help you sort out the mess of credit-hour requirements that will undoubtedly haunt you for the rest of your college days. Not sure if that government class counts toward your political-science track? Wondering if you can substitute your AP scores for introductory science classes? Departmental advisors can give you answers to these kinds of questions, but you're going to have to ask them first.

Once you choose a major, you'll probably be assigned to an advisor from that department. While policy on this varies from school to school, you should try to make sure that your advisor's specialty is as close to your intended focus of study as possible. As your academic years progress, the issues you face become more and more complex—where to concentrate within your major, what to write your thesis about, where to apply to graduate school—and you'll need to have an advisor who knows a great deal about very particular problems. You should also try to find an advisor with whom you get along personally. You won't be interacting with this person too often but this is an important resource and a valuable relationship for you.

Whatever you do, don't settle for subpar advising. If your advisor seems confused or uninformed, pay a few discreet visits to other advisors in the department. You might find someone who's more willing to help, or is more receptive to your way of doing things. If your school allows it, switch to this advisor as soon as possible. Above all, be honest about your needs and concerns. Let your old advisor know why you're going elsewhere and give specific reasons whenever you can. He or she may not appreciate being dumped (who would?), but you won't leave room for argument if you come prepared.

We Talk With . . .
Brian, Senior, Brown University

What advice would you offer to college students about choosing a major?

My advice is to pick your major based on the classes you like taking, not based on what you want to be when you grow up. If you don't like political science, you shouldn't be President. Likewise, if you don't like "Exotic Dancing 101," then perhaps you should reconsider being a stripper.

My first two years, I took at least one cool class in each of the fields I was interested in: media, theatre, American studies, education, English, Spanish. It was like eight-minute dating—except with more books and less nervous laughter. In the end, I learned that majors are like middle-school cliques, only they can't reject you for someone prettier. Choose based on the people whom you want to sit in class/at the lunch table with. Meeting alumni in my major who have cool jobs out in the real world helped reassure my decision because I could see who I would end up being.

If you were doing it all over again, what would you do differently when choosing a major?

I would triple major. It's the only way to outdo those under-achieving double majors. Besides, my social life was getting in the way of valuable study time.

But seriously, I'd reconsider concentrating in art/semiotics, which is a combination of my actual major and visual arts. I decided against it last minute because I didn't want to spend the rest of my life explaining to people what "semiotics" was.

4

Finding Your Passion Outside of Class

Sometimes you have to get out of class to pursue your interests and discover new ones. Say you really enjoyed working on your high school paper and are thinking about a career in journalism after graduation. Working with your college newspaper will teach you more about reporting and newspaper publishing than any English class could ever do. Or perhaps you're thinking of becoming a player in the Washington political scene after graduation? Combine your major in political science with a leadership position in student government and you've got the full package.

To inspire you to test out your old interests and chase new passions, we've devoted the bulk of this chapter to the many ways you can get involved in your college organizations and activities. By no means have we included every possibility— not even close—but hopefully we've whet your appetite and halfway through this chapter you'll be on your way to joining that club or organization you've always been curious about. And who knows, your quest to find a major might just get a little easier after you do.

- Where Do I Sign Up?
- There's a First Time for Everything
- The College Times
- Broadcast the Night Away
- Acting Up
- Give Back to the Community
- It's Up to You to Change the World
- Nominate Yourself

Where Do I Sign Up?

 Adults Weigh In

In many ways, college is all about self-discovery. There's got to be something out there that you want to do with your life, right? For a lot of people, it involves something other than history or philosophy, something that you can't be taught in the classroom and the only way to find it is to turn to extracurriculars.

—Chaplain
Guilford College

When you first show up at college as a wide-eyed freshman, the sheer amount of opportunities available to you can be overwhelming. Don't worry though—after a while you'll find where you fit in.

—Junior
Harvard University

Getting oriented in the extracurricular scene at college can seem like quite a daunting task. How do you know what's out there? How do you get involved? What will you have to do and what sort of commitments will you have to make? It turns out that most organizations and groups are always looking for people to add their talents to the mix and they greet newbies with open arms. Once you have your foot in the door, people will be emailing you all the time to give you the 411, and before you know it you'll be having the time of your life. Or you'll be realizing that getting up at 4:00 am for your radio broadcast is less fun than you thought and you'll look for other ways to express your political views.

Take some time to check out the many options that are available at your school. This can be a relatively straightforward task, but at some larger schools you'll have to work to get your finger on the pulse of the sorts of things you could do. Either way, it's definitely worth looking into all of your available options, since you never know what sort of crazy activity your school might have that you'll fall in love with.

Many colleges have activity fairs at the start of each school year or semester where representatives from various student groups have booths from which they dispense fliers, copies of their latest printed project (if they have one), and, of course, valuable pieces of information. Many organizations will even hold information meetings or question-and-answer sessions at their offices. Attending these events is a great way not only to learn about what's out there, but also to meet the organizers and members of these groups.

Adults Weigh In

Whether you're at a large school or a small school, it's crucial that as a freshman, you take the initiative to get involved outside of the classroom. For students who say they don't know how to get involved, keep in mind that it's unlikely that anyone is going to knock on your dorm room door and ask you to join a club or play a sport. It's easy to stay in your room and Instant Message friends from high school, but that's a death knell. Pick several organizations of interest and attend some meetings. Then, decide what you like best and make choices about how you will spend your time outside of class.

—Dean of Students
Washington and Lee University

There's a First Time for Everything

One of my biggest regrets about college is not having tried enough different activities. This is so much harder to do after graduation when you have to think about things like paying rent and finding a job. But in college I had the chance to do many things without much risk and I didn't take full advantage of it.

—Recent Grad
Wesleyan University

Even if you think that you know exactly what you want to do for the rest of your life, try a few different things—you never know what might pique your interest. If you don't like a certain activity, you can always go back to the safety of what you know and love to do. But you might also discover a whole new side of yourself and a whole new direction for your college life and future.

Don't shy away from trying things in which you have absolutely no experience. If you've never acted but want to give it a try, go and audition. The worst-case scenario is that you don't get the part. If you have no journalism experience but want to work for the college paper, do it anyway. This is your chance to get experience, and even though some campus organizations might seem extremely professional, you probably won't need many (if any) credentials to get involved.

There's no place where it's easier to take risks and try new things than in college. If you like your new activity, great! If you hate it, you can quit and not commit yourself to anything. Take a chance and you might surprise yourself.

Taking Detours

by Holly, Senior,
New York University

When I first got to school, I was a communications major and was all set for a career as a newspaper columnist. As a freshman, I joined the school newspaper as an arts and entertainment writer. After a semester, I was promoted to editor, which was quite thrilling. After a year of doing this sort of work, however, I began to realize that perhaps my heart was not in the job after all.

I went out and joined the Student Government Association, thinking a little campus politics was more what I needed. I switched my major to history and began to think about a career in politics. However, I found the wheels very slow in turning and decided to look for myself elsewhere.

I then became a philosophy major and joined the Philosophy Club. I submerged myself in the philosophical world, wondering what the purpose of life was. I even transferred schools to be at one of the top philosophy programs. And now the majority of my philosophical pursuits include questions such as: "How on earth am I going to pay off my loans by being a door-to-door philosopher?"

I have now come full circle and re-emerged as a journalist doing an internship at NBC, but I've kept my philosophy major and my history minor, and I'm starting work this summer in an intensive journalism course. I've learned a very valuable lesson: When your college courses aren't helping you find yourself, it's best to turn to the world of extracurricular clubs and jobs to see what the real applications of your interests are all about.

The College Times

We Talk With . . .

Ellen, Freshman, Brown University

Have you discovered an interest or passion through getting involved outside of class?
Yes! I've been writing for the *Brown Daily Herald*, our campus newspaper, and recently became a staff writer.

How has getting involved beyond the classroom impacted your college experience?

Writing for the *Herald* gives me the sense that I'm making a contribution—both to campus and to the community. Also, I've met others who are interested in writing and have become friends with them.

I think it's essential that all students get involved with something outside of classes, whether sports, arts, or political or religious groups, as early as possible in their college careers. The campus can be a large and lonely place as a freshman, and having something to belong to can do a lot to stave off homesickness. Besides, it's a great way to make new friends.

Like Nike says—Just Do It. So what if you've never tried it before? So what if you're not sure you can? College is a great place to test out new activities and find what you love.

Have you discovered a potential career path by getting involved?

Getting involved with the *Herald* has gotten me interested in the field of journalism, something I'd like to pursue after graduation. Thanks to my great experience with our paper, I'm looking into journalism internships for next summer.

If you want to be a journalist, join your college newspaper. These publications train you for the job in ways that classes can't. As a college reporter, you are thrown into the trenches and must learn to do the job by yourself. It's a great place to get clips and a safe place to make those inevitable mistakes.

—Senior
San Diego State University

You can learn how to write well in your English class, but it won't give you a taste for what it's like to work for a newspaper—writing a thesis paper and reporting on a story are two very different things. Your college newspaper or magazine, however, is the perfect place to test out or gain some journalistic skills. Every college has numerous campus papers, magazines, and other publications. Some are published daily, some weekly or monthly. Countless Pulitzer Prize–winning journalists and cartoonists got their start at their college papers, and there's no reason you can't follow in their footsteps.

The most obvious way for you to get involved with your school publication is to work as a reporter. As a newshound, you would get to attend cool speeches and events thanks to your press pass, interview interesting and famous people in the area, talk to many of your classmates, and have your writing smack on the front page of the paper. (Well, maybe not right away.) Papers can never have too many reporters, and if you

 Mike's Corner

When I entered college, I enjoyed comedy about as much as the next person, but I didn't have any experience writing it. But when I started writing my own comedy for the school's humor magazine, I became obsessed with it, and now I plan to try to make a living out of it. If I hadn't attended the introductory meeting for the magazine on a whim, who knows what I would want to do with the rest of my life? If you enjoy writing, definitely check out the 'zine scene at your school because you never know when you're going to become obsessed with something you didn't really have the opportunity to do in high school.

love the idea of being the one to break the story of the crazy philosophy professor who earned tenure for revolutionizing metaphysics, there's no better job for you.

If the idea of researching and reporting news stories doesn't sound that appealing to you, keep in mind that you can do all sorts of different jobs for a college publication. For example, as an editorial columnist, you'd get to speak your mind about current events on campus and in the real world. Jobs like this are much harder to come by than those for reporters, so be prepared to make a good case for why you have something interesting and unique to say.

If you plan on attending every one of your school's football games, consider working as a sportswriter. If you like the idea of getting into plays, concerts, and movies for free, receiving free CDs to review, and maybe even interviewing a celebrity or two, try your hand as an arts and entertainment columnist.

I've always been a die-hard sports fan, so it was only natural that I'd continue to chase that passion in college. I worked as a beat reporter for a few teams and it was a great way for me to improve my journalistic skills while writing about something I loved.

—Recent Grad
Wesleyan University

If you're interested in the business side of publishing your campus publications offer tons of ways to get your hands dirty. There are usually several business managers in charge of different aspects of the publication, such as an advertising manager who works with on- and off-campus organizations to sell ads, and a circulation manager who ensures that the paper boy goes through his entire delivery route. If you're looking for this kind of business experience, working on a campus publication is a great way to find it and enhance your résumé. It's also a unique way to get an education in how publications are run and organized, which is extremely useful if you're considering journalism or publishing after graduation.

> I think that by just working on the student newspaper for a semester you can learn more than taking classes for four years. This is a great way to really get a taste of what the media world is like.
>
> —Junior
> Seton Hall University

Broadcast the Night Away

We Talk With . . .

Mandel, Recent Grad, Harvard University, Former Vice President of Harvard-Radcliffe Television (HRTV), Manager of Development at Fremantle Media

Why did you join HRTV?

I've always had an interest in television. I did a sketch comedy show in high school very similar to the one I ended up developing and producing for HRTV. I figured it would be a great way for me to expand upon what I did in high school. What particularly drew me in was that a game show was being produced for HRTV. Being a huge game-show fan, I felt that it was a great

opportunity to produce something in one of my all-time favorite genres.

What sort of impact did your time with HRTV have on your
college experience?
It was a great way to get my mind off the stress and tedium of
classes. I also met some of my best friends in college through
HRTV. It was one of the few places where I could really let
loose and have the freedom to do the types of shows that I
wanted to.

How did joining HRTV help you prepare for achieving your
professional goals?
I was able to apply a lot of things I did with the productions of
HRTV shows to the work I've done in the TV biz out here on the
West Coast. My work producing my own game show especially
helped in the work I've done with developing game shows for
Dick Clark Productions and Fremantle Media. I really didn't realize it until I moved out here, but HRTV really was a great training ground for the productions with which I've been involved
after graduation.

College radio stations have a long and storied tradition of
boasting the most eclectic and well-chosen playlists in the country. If you're a music buff who loves to show off your gigantic
collection of opera, zydeco, and grunge-rock CDs to anyone
who will pay attention to you, give DJing at your university station a serious look. Most stations offer you time slots where
you can play pretty much whatever music you want (even if you
have to start out with the 2:00 am to 6:00 am shift).

Of course, there's a lot more you can do at a radio station
than just play music. Most also have news and sports shows

or segments. Some have live talk shows where the host or a panel moderates political discussions or gives advice to callers. These shows range in theme from straightforward discussions about national politics to heated debates over who's going to win the NCAA West Regional Semifinals game to "Loveline"-esque dating advice. There are even comedy shows, and most stations are pretty flexible about letting students start their own if they have a unique enough idea. And as a perk, lots of bands stop by the local college station when they're in town for an interview or a short set, so you might get to rub shoulders with a bunch of famous rock stars.

> When it comes to Babson College Radio, it's not just my passion for being a part of this budding station that makes being general manager special, but it's the ethic that comes from the passion. As life proves, when a person finds something they care about deeply, he or she will give all they can to make this newfound joy successful. Plus, college radio is not just a stepping-stone to the real world, but it's a place for "different" people like myself to show the world what they can do.
>
> —Senior
> Babson College

If you're interested in broadcasting, you should also think about getting involved with your college TV station. Most of them broadcast over dorm cable or over local community stations, and thus beam the work of the television crew right into everyone's room. If your show is successful, you'll have people all over campus tuning in every week to see your latest episode.

While not every school has its own television station, those that do offer tons of possible shows on which you can work.

For example, lots of stations run sketch comedy shows or even sitcoms if you'd like to try your hand at writing or acting out funny things. There are news and student-life shows for the photojournalists out there, which can contain anything from discussions over university politics to footage from last Friday's celebration in the quad after the football team beat its rival.

Every episode of a television show involves a lot of production, so there are lots of different areas with which you can get involved. All shows require some sort of actors or hosts, a staff of writers, a director to guide the action, and a camera crew to film it. Once all the footage is taped and goes to post-production, an editor will be needed to piece the show together. This sounds like a lot of jobs, and it is—and each one is an opportunity for you to get involved and learn something new and different.

With all the freedom that comes along with having a camera and your own weekly time slot, college TV organizations offer you the chance to explore almost any one of your interests. Especially useful if your school doesn't have a strong communications department, working for your college TV station will give you a strong foundation in the basics of television production, invaluable to anyone who is considering entering this field after college.

Unless your school has an unusually strong communications program, you likely won't have the opportunity to explore your interest in broadcast media inside the classroom. Working at a radio or TV station, however, will teach you how to apply your interest in music and broadcasting to developing skills that might actually help you find an awesome job in the field when you graduate.

Mike's Corner

One of my favorite parts of working on college television shows was the chance to be involved with so many different aspects of production. I was able to find out not only how exactly the different pieces fit together to create the final product, but I also discovered which aspects were my favorite.

We Talk With . . .

Steven, Recent Grad,
Harvard University, Writer for
"The Late Show with David Letterman"
and former president of the
Harvard Lampoon

Why did you join the humor magazine, the Harvard Lampoon?
I joined the *Harvard Lampoon* because it seemed like far and away the coolest thing at Harvard, a school not particularly famous for being fun. The *Lampoon*'s long history of pranks and parties, whimsical buildings, secretive traditions, and a hilarious magazine all combined to make it seem like something I'd really like to be a part of.

What sort of impact has your time with the Lampoon had on your college experience?
My time at the *Lampoon* was, in some important ways, my college experience. I joined during the first semester of my freshman year and put a lot of time into it right up until I graduated. I made some great friends, sharpened my focus

on comedy writing, and had a wonderful time. Certainly, when I look back at college, my fondest memories will almost all involve the *Lampoon*.

How did joining the Lampoon *help you prepare for achieving your professional goals?*
Working on the *Lampoon*, in addition to being super fun, was great training for a writing career. Being around dozens of extremely funny, extremely talented writers gave me a chance to develop my instincts, see how the process of developing comedy works, and experiment with comedy ideas and writing styles. This was great preparation for trying to find a job in the tough world of professional comedy writing.

Acting Up

Do you feel at home on the stage? Are you at your best when a packed auditorium watches in awe as you deliver the final lines of a *Hamlet* soliloquy, play a solo from one of Beethoven's symphonies, or leap in the air and spin 360 degrees before you land in the arms of your dance partner?

If so, you shouldn't have too much trouble finding a forum at college to indulge yourself. Whether you enjoy performing plays, music, or dance moves, you'll find plenty of students and locals who will crowd themselves into a theater to watch you. And if you've never actually tried your hand at performing but have this undeniable urge to try, do it. This isn't Broadway and you don't have to have any kind of acting experience. Brave the auditions, let your talents loose, and if you can't make it on the first try, try again.

If you're interested in pursuing a performance career after college—Hollywood, anyone?—there is no better way to get practice, toughen up your ego, and figure out which direction you might want to go in than by getting involved with campus theater, a dance company, or another type of performance troupe. Or perhaps you're thinking of becoming a theater

Dancing at College

by Duygu, Sophomore, Brown University

I went to dance shows for years. I would sit there at the front of the audience spellbound by the performance. Then, I came to Brown, where I was given an opportunity to try what I was used to watching. I thought it would be a fun extracurricular activity, nothing more than that. I was yet to discover how much more important it would become.

After some time with a dance troupe, I could do some of the "fancy" moves, and soon I was promoted from spectator to dancer. My time rehearsing started to make me feel better about myself. I enjoyed it more and more each day.

After my first semester at Brown, I was still undecided about my major. Seeing that I really enjoy dancing, I thought maybe I could study something to do with it. What looked like only some sort of an activity was now a possible option for my major. I took choreography my second semester and loved it. I feel like through learning new steps and techniques as part of the ballroom dance club, I was able to understand myself better.

I might or might not decide to become a theater arts major, but at least now I have a better understanding of what kind of stuff I can do well and what I really enjoy.

major and going on to work behind the scenes of Broadway productions? Put your interests to the test and get some invaluable practice by becoming a stage manager/set designer/lighting coordinator for a campus theater production.

Give Back to the Community

To know that given a different set of circumstances, I could be the one without enough to eat, without a place to live, without hope, makes me feel obligated to help those who are less fortunate.

—Senior

James Madison University

Whether you want to devote two or forty hours a week to it, working in public service is probably one of the most fulfilling extracurriculars you can take up at college.

The list of possible opportunities to get involved is almost endless. If you'd like to work with children, you can tutor or mentor kids from disadvantaged backgrounds or with disabilities in an after-school program to help them gain confidence, prepare them for the challenges of middle school/high school/college, and just give them stable relationships with people they can look up to. For example, a program at one college sends students to play and teach music to children at schools that can't afford music programs. If you're interested in working with children after graduation, get involved with one of these types of programs and see what the experience might be like.

There is a middle ground between partying four nights a week and living in the library: It's called extracurricular activities. For me, volunteering was the outlet I needed to have fun without being hung over the next morning. The volunteer opportunities at college are endless. I love kids, so I tutor a little boy twice a week and help out at a school for autistic children. Volunteering has proved to be a rewarding break from classes and studying.

—Freshman
Emory University

You can also work with adults, of course. For example, you can teach English to recent immigrants in the community. You could work with individuals with disabilities, the mentally ill, victims of domestic violence, and the homeless in any number of capacities, from the group's organizer to a volunteer. You could become active with your local Habitat for Humanity chapter and help build or renovate affordable houses for those living in poverty. You could help staff a crisis hotline for members of the community or for students at your own school. Nursing homes are always looking for volunteers to talk to or perform for the elderly as well. If you're interested in medicine, you might be able to volunteer at a local hospital or teach CPR to members of the community.

During my freshman year I taught English to a Vietnamese immigrant. He was a doctor back at home, but was only able to work as a janitor in America because he hardly spoke any English. He made some progress during our sessions, but most of all, I think, he was able to get some hope that he could eventually learn enough English to go back to medicine.

—Recent Grad
Wesleyan University

Becoming a leader or an officer in a service organization at college is a great way to develop the administrative skills you would need to assume such a role after you graduate. Even if you don't plan to pursue community service after college, working within the community will give you valuable experience that will help you in whatever you plan to do with the rest of your life. Not to mention it's the perfect way to contribute something to the community around your campus and perhaps change a life or two for the better.

> The Newman Club at Trinity College has helped me adjust to the hectic lifestyle of a college student and has grounded my understanding of what an active member of an institution of higher learning should be doing, both on campus and in the surrounding community. Community service groups put into action the concepts of social justice and basic human rights that can sometimes remain just ideas in a student's notebook.
>
> —Junior
> Trinity College

It's Up to You to Change the World

Adults Weigh In

As a higher education professional, I attribute a lot of my own personal development and growth to the experiences that I've had outside of the traditional classroom. In fact, I don't know if I would have even found my way into a career as a student affairs professional if not for my extracurricular involvement both as an undergraduate and graduate student. As an individual who works closely with students and student groups in an advisory capacity, and as someone who hires staff—many of whom are recent graduates—I cannot say enough about how important it is for undergraduates to become engaged in extracurricular activities. So much of what makes a person successful in today's world has to do with his or her ability to function competently in a multicultural society, to communicate effectively, and to exercise leadership ethically. Seldom are these abilities taught in the classroom—they are more than likely acquired through the triumphs and failures one undergoes in peer-on-peer interactions.

—Dean of Students
University of Wisconsin–Madison

When you were in elementary school, did you make it your lifelong goal to help save the whales or eliminate land mines? Now that you're in college, stay true to that goal by joining or founding a political activist group! When a bunch of college students put their minds to it, they can really make things happen.

There are, of course, tons of political issues on the table that you might want to fight for. For example, you could join your school's Amnesty International chapter to free political prisoners and fight for human rights all over the globe. You could work to change unjust labor laws in America or overseas (close down those sweatshops!). If you have a stance on the issue of abortion, both pro-choice and pro-life groups exist at a number of schools, and they sometimes hold public debates. Some students fight to reduce handgun violence, while others fight to protect our right to bear arms. You could join a student organization that draws attention to social problems, such as those that push for racial equality or promote research into terrible diseases such as AIDS. You could give in to the tree-hugger in you and work to defend the environment, or endangered species. The possibilities are truly endless.

Working with a college activist group does more than just give you a taste of what activism is about and allow you to meet other students who share your stance on important issues. These organizations actually do make a difference, both in drawing national and international media attention and affecting real social change. College groups have been able to raise substantial amounts of money for their causes and gather hundreds, if not thousands, of signatures for petitions. Every year, thousands of Amnesty International letters that serve as an important vehicle for putting pressure on oppressive regimes are written by college students.

I've learned a great deal by participating in the University of Delaware's Students for the Environment. It has shown me a bigger picture of the environmental movement as a whole while giving me the opportunity to learn and discuss environmental concerns with my peers. I've also had the opportunity to attend conferences and listen to amazing speakers on a range of topics. Being a leader in an organization such as this has provided both frustration (when other people don't understand our passion for the environment) and satisfaction (when an event goes well and we can share in our concern for mother nature). It's hard these days to connect with people since our lives have become so hectic, but a group like this one can easily provide many opportunities for building relationships with others who have similar interests.

—Junior
University of Delaware

Voice your mind, get involved, make a difference, and learn something! College is such an ideal time to do this and to explore the issues you care about, as well as to find some new ones that may become your passion.

Nominate Yourself

The Joys of Model United Nations

by Selesa, Senior, Columbia University

I joined Model United Nations at Columbia because I did debate in high school and wanted to continue with it in college. As part of Model United Nations, I represent a specific country at conferences at other colleges where we have parliamentary-style debates about a range of topics.

My first debate was particularly exciting. I was scared to death to be competing at the college level, but government simulations lend themselves more to camaraderie than competition because diplomacy is important and because everyone's working toward finding a solution to the same problem, so it ended up being really relaxed. It was less like a debate and more like a symposium.

I've had the opportunity to debate some particularly exciting topics as well. For example, once my committee discussed transnational organized crime, specifically the Chinese Triads, Japanese Yakuza, Sicilian Mafia, and Colombian drug cartels.

Model United Nations has not been a huge time commitment. I occasionally go to weekly meetings just to see how people are doing, but I usually only participate in the conferences, which happen about once a month.

> My experiences dealing with the simulated bureaucracy of Model United Nations have shown me that I do *not* want to become a representative in a large governmental organization. If I ever get involved in politics, it would definitely be at a grassroots level.

Are you an overeager political science major who is disappointed that you have to wait until you're thirty-five before you can run for president? Do you tape C-SPAN while you're at class so you can keep up with the latest debates over domestic financial policy? If so, you'll be excited to know that there are lots of ways to improve your political savvy at college outside of your comparative politics class.

You can join a partisan organization and directly advance your political leanings or get involved in student government and get a taste of power. Alternatively, you could join a group that puts on governmental simulation conferences or run for student government and influence the policies that affect student life at your school. All of these are more fun and exciting options than watching recordings in your C-SPAN tape library for the umpteenth time. And you can learn a lot more from them, too.

One of the most direct ways to become involved with politics at your campus is to join a partisan club. While many schools have a College Democrats or College Republicans club, you can find (or start) clubs devoted to stances all over the political spectrum. By working with these groups, you'll not only meet a bunch of people who share your point of view, but also get to work for your political cause in a number of capacities that will teach you about politics and political organizations. If you're thinking about a career in politics of any flavor, joining one of these groups is a great way to get some experience and a true taste—although on a smaller scale—of what it might be like.

> Participating in the College Democrats has served as an outlet for me to see the interaction between theory and actual policy. As a member of a political club, you can make a difference in the real-world application of the things you learn about in class.
>
> —Senior
> Georgetown University School of Foreign Service

Are you interested in politics and government and how all of those complicated political structures are organized? Would you like the chance to role-play with a bunch of your friends in business suits? If so, you're in luck because many colleges put on or attend annual conferences where both college and high school students simulate the duties of various government bodies. While this might sound kind of strange to the uninitiated, the conferences are actually a lot of fun.

> It's odd to think that I came to college almost completely for academics, and I have spent more time this semester helping to run the Yale International Relations Association (YIRA) and our Model United Nations conferences than I have on my classwork. When I think about what makes my experience worthwhile, I of course note how much I've learned about international politics, diplomacy, and how to accommodate conflicting preferences, but I know the most rewarding part of my involvement in YIRA is the friends I've made.
>
> —Junior
> Yale University

Currently, several different types of simulation programs exist at colleges. Both Model Senate and Model Congress programs deal with strictly American issues, while Model Organization of American States, Model Arab League, and Model Organization of African Unity incorporate other countries as well. Participants in the granddaddy of all simulations, Model United Nations, represent delegates from all around the world. If you're interested, check to see if your college has an on-campus group that travels to these simulations or organize one yourself. By getting this type of experience you're given first-hand exposure to the ins and outs of the political system, as well as the hot topics actually debated in Washington and across the world.

And if you can't wait until after graduation to start bossing people around in an official capacity, definitely consider student government. Student government members do all sorts of things. Many are in charge of providing certain services to students, such as organizing shuttles to popular off-campus destinations or coordinating online book exchanges. Most also work to improve the quality of student life by urging the administration to renovate the gym or improve the crummy dining-hall food, for example. Some discuss academic issues with the administration, by arguing over the qualifications of teaching assistants or the necessity of a core academic curriculum. Most allocate funding for other student groups, thereby holding the ultimate power over them.

Working in student government can be a blast and it gives you a chance to practice your diplomacy while you make things happen that actually affect the quality of life at college.

Adults Weigh In

Extracurricular involvement brings to life what you learn in the classroom and provides you with opportunities to apply classroom learning in real-life settings. Through extracurricular involvement, students learn to set goals, work as part of an organization, develop the ability to compromise, and develop leadership skills. Employers tell us that they want to hire students who have been involved outside of the classroom because they bring good "people skills" and a sense of citizenship to their roles.

—Associate Vice President for Campus Life and Dean of
Students, University of Arizona

Finding Your Passion
by Terray, Junior,
Middlebury College

Finding your passion in college is simple. There are two things you must do. First, tweak your mind. Forget that your future, the success of your life as you know it, the happiness of progeny, and the honor of your family hinge upon what you make of your college career; they don't. Your undergraduate years are not a means to an end. Even though you have likely spent all of high school preparing for college so that your college career will prepare you for life, college is not yet one more opportunity to spend tailoring yourself for a future that will probably never arrive. College is an end in itself, and it bursts with potential. Enjoy this time and take advantage of it.

Second, try a bit of everything. If you're already devoted to a source of meaning, you would not be reading this book. Thus, it is important to sample everything that tickles your fancy. When you find the right area you will feel an urge to read around the assignments. You will realize that you enjoy thinking about your papers or problems sets in your free time, and you'll ultimately find that what you are studying feels like it is a portion of yourself.

5

Starting Your Own Group

So what if your college or university doesn't offer a club or an organization where you can pursue and develop your interests. Or, perhaps, your college does have a group you want to join, but you can't for whatever reason (such as when the only a cappella group at your school rejects you on the final night of auditions).

Don't sweat it. Instead, start your own group! While this might seem like a daunting prospect, bear in mind that every club on your campus was started by *somebody*. When you create your own activity, you get to shape it to your goals and watch it blossom and grow. Starting something from scratch is extremely rewarding and if you have an entrepreneurial streak in you, this is the perfect way to put it to work.

So, how about it?

- Draw Up the Blueprints
- The More the Merrier
- Rules of Engagement
- Cutting Through Red Tape
- After You're Gone

Draw Up the Blueprints

First things first: Before you can go about advertising for your group's first free concert, whipping up some brownies for a fund-raising bake sale, or holding the first meeting of your dream organization, you need to figure out what exactly your group will *do*.

Say you want to start an a cappella group. You've got a few initial questions to ask yourself, such as:

✓ What sort of music will you perform?
✓ How many members will the group have, and will the group be coed or single sex?
✓ How many hours a week will you expect the other singers to commit to the group?

While you may not need to figure out every single detail at this stage (such as what color shirts you'll wear when you perform), you should at least try to sketch out an organizational structure, and, most importantly, ask yourself why you're starting the group in the first place.

If there are other similar organizations on campus, be sure to make clear the ways in which yours is different. Perhaps you're interested in journalism but find that the main campus weekly focuses too much on what's happening at the university while you want to publish more editorials on national politics. Or maybe you want to play in a pops orchestra and the existing orchestra has a conductor who only wants to perform classical symphonies.

Don't feel like you need to write up a formal mission statement or something extremely complicated. Just know enough so that you can tell people who might want to join what they will get to do as members, what will be expected from them, and why your group will be so awesome that they have to join.

One great way to search for ideas for groups is to look at the websites of extracurricular organizations at other colleges. There's always some unique group at a school across the

 Mike's Corner

I had a great time shaping the goals of the a cappella group in which I was a founding member. While most groups on campus performed Top-40 pop music, I'm really into indie rock music, and arranged a bunch of songs in that genre for our group to perform. It would've been harder to get an older group more laden in tradition to perform songs considered unconventional by a cappella standards, so I'm glad that I entered this group when I did.

country that does something interesting. Don't feel like you have to copy any group's philosophy and objectives, but this is a good way to come up with ideas.

This first step of creating your own group may seem intimidating, and you might be afraid that it will fail or become a horrible disaster. While it's certainly possible that things won't work out exactly the way you want them to, there is no harm in trying. At worst, you'll waste a chunk of your free time and have a solid experience of starting something original under your belt. At best, you'll have a really fun and fulfilling outlet that will introduce you to some of your best friends and will affect the lives of many students in the future.

The More the Merrier

Once you know what you want out of your creation, you'll need to get some other people on board. If you're afraid you'll have trouble raising interest for the Swahili Club you want to found, don't sweat it. College students (especially freshmen) will try anything, and even if you don't think your school is large enough, there are probably more people than you imagine who will show up at your introductory meeting. You just have to let them know that your group exists and then pique their interest, which is quite a formidable challenge.

There are dozens of different ways to get the attention of your classmates. The most obvious is to put up catchy posters all over campus. Make sure that your poster grabs

Mike's Corner

One very effective way to recruit people is to hand out small fliers that have the relevant info at a well-traveled location. In my experience, camping out in front of a dining hall is a great way to get a lot of people to know about your group—everyone's got to come and eat at some point!

the attention of those who walk past it by using large, exciting fonts or fun images. Don't simply announce the existence of your club in twelve point New Times Roman, or no one will take the time to give your posters a second look. Your poster should be brief and include the time and place of the first meeting for your group. The idea is to catch people's attention and give them a clear explanation of what they can do to get involved.

You could also try to attract attention by sending out emails to people you think might be interested. You should avoid emailing hundreds of strangers, since sending unsolicited emails might be considered harassment at some schools. A better idea is to email your friends and ask them to forward your email to anyone who they might think will be interested in your idea.

Running a blurb in a campus publication or having a story written about your group is another tried and true method. Talk to an editor or a student reporter and see if you can't interest them in writing a story—however short—about your initiative.

One of the best ways to spread the word is by telling as many people as you know about your efforts to get your group going. Word of mouth gets around quicker than any email.

You'll probably want to hold an information session or introductory meeting where you can explain what you want to do with this group and listen to ideas other people might have about directions and activities. Be as prepared as possible for this meeting so that you can impress potential new members and convince them to join. Keep it short, informal, and think about what you're going to say ahead of time. It's a good idea to print out some fliers conveying the purpose of the group along with your contact information, and be sure to pass out a sign-up sheet so you can collect the names and email addresses of your new members.

If the nature of your organization is such that you can't take everyone who is interested in working with you, keep in mind that you'll probably need to hold some sort of audition. For example, if you want to start a theatrical troupe, you'll have to plan ahead and prepare some scripts and guidelines for the acting audition process. Try to bring in some other people to help you so you can do a better job evaluating talent. Also, be prepared for the difficult job of turning people away. It's best to tell people in person or on the phone that they didn't make the cut, and consider giving them advice in case they want to try out again in the future. This can help ease the bitterness they feel toward your group, particularly if some of them are your friends or people you know.

Founding the U.N.C. Barbeque Club

by William, Senior,
University of North Carolina

Ever since my friends have had cars here at school, we've been going to barbecue restaurants to eat. In the Carolinas, barbecue restaurants specialize in a dish simply called "barbecue," which consists of chopped up pork with a vinegar, tomato, or mustard sauce. The extent of my love of this food is such that I was once embarrassingly late to leave on a retreat because I decided to drive out to a barbecue restaurant. What we liked about these restaurants was the culture, community, and traditions that were unique to each place, as well as the excellent food.

I realized that most of us going on these trips were out-of-state students or from a few of the very large cities in North Carolina, so we created the club to introduce people to different cultures and communities around the state. The club has been a real success, as we now have approximately 140 members, including students, faculty, staff, administrative officials, and others across the East Coast. We are an officially recognized student organization, and we meet about once a month. At the meeting, when we go to a restaurant, we bring along experts to talk to the group about the modern American South. Some of our past speakers have been writers, poets, political analysts, sociologists, and, of course, chefs.

We publicize meetings on our electronic listserv, but most members hear about us through word of mouth. However, we also occasionally man a table at the central area for students on campus, sell T-shirts to promote the club, and maintain a website to keep people informed about events.

Rules of Engagement

First things first: Who's going to be in charge of buying the beer?

—Recent Grad
Denison College

So now you have a bunch of other students on your hands who can't wait to start visiting homeless shelters or preparing invitations for law professors to come speak at campus. Great! But what are you going to do with them?

At this early stage in the development of your group, you need to fill in the details of its structure. First, come up with an officer core:

✓ Do you need a president, and are you going to take that responsibility? What is the president going to do, anyway?
✓ Do you need a vice president?
✓ How about a secretary, treasurer, publicity manager, editorial chair, business manager, music director, faculty liaison, or what have you? Which positions do you need, and exactly what will they all do?

Consider modeling your group's executive board after those implemented by other organizations on campus, or feel free to do your own thing. You don't need to create all of these positions, of course, and it's definitely better to have less bureaucracy than more. Figure out what has to be done and then assign people roles that correspond to those responsibilities.

Next, work out the details of how your group will go about doing what it does. For example:

✓ Will you meet weekly, biweekly, or every evening?
✓ What types of events will you plan?
✓ Where will you broadcast your television show?
✓ How will you get the magazine printed up?
✓ Where can you reserve practice space?
✓ What advertisers will you solicit to pay for production costs?
✓ Are members expected to practice outside of rehearsal?

These are just a few examples for different groups—you'll need to come with your own. One useful technique is to focus on achieving a specific goal—organizing your first protest, publishing your first magazine issue, holding your first outdoor concert, etc.—and then figuring out what needs to be done to achieve it. Focusing on doing something concrete keeps everyone organized and saves you from arguing over vague details like whether you'll have five annual events/issues/protests or one.

If you're new to the extracurricular jungle, you might find that there are a lot more details to attend to than you would think were possible. Try not to get too bogged down in details and expect some bumps along the way. It's important to remember to remain flexible as you get started; listen and ask for suggestions from other people in your group. No one likes being told what to do and even though this is your idea and you're the leader, getting input and making people feel like they're contributing will make things run much more smoothly.

Structuring the "Harvard Lowkeys"

by Sue, Senior, Harvard University

Once I had singers in the a cappella group I started, everything from the group's mission, officers, and everyday logistics had to be worked out. I realized from the beginning that to make the group run smoothly, I had to be willing to do everything, from business managing to music directing to publicity. Since the group was suddenly fourteen instead of one, however, I had to listen to the variety of opinions and ideas on how the group should be run. Everyone agreed that the group needed a music director, business manager, and president, based upon the model of the other a cappella groups.

Many of the positions that followed were created in response to new situations, and the positions were constantly reinvented according to group dynamic. It was decided that an Assistant Music Director was necessary to take over when the Music Director was not available, and was a good way to train younger members to eventually lead the group's musical life. At one point, most of the group was dissatisfied with the way the group was being run musically, and voted to install a four-person musical team. This proved to be ponderous by the next semester, and was quickly done away with.

I realized after a few years that all the constant changes in the group were absolutely natural; after all, new members were being inducted each semester, and old members left all the time to focus on other things. The dynamic changed rapidly, and the older group members realized that the most important mission, goal, and duty that we could encourage in our officers was that of diplomacy, lightheartedness, and a desire to satisfy every member of the current incarnation of the group.

Cutting Through Red Tape

Finally, you're having the time of your life running your own mock-trial team or a cappella group or whatever group you've started—your dream has truly become a reality. Now, you want to host a tournament of local college teams at your school, but you don't know where the competition could take place. Or, even worse, you have a tournament in Florida next week and the group spent all the money it earned at the bake sale when it hosted that kegger last Friday. Who do you turn to now?

Fear not—the university administration might be able to help you! It's worth getting to know the dean in charge of collegiate extracurriculars (or whatever the equivalent position is at your school) as soon as possible because he or she will likely be able to hook you up with resources you never knew existed. If you're lucky, this person will tell you when you can book the lecture halls in the science center for your tournament and show you how to apply for loads of grant money. Find out who is in charge of pulling strings and get to know that person as well as possible.

Many times, dealing with the administration is nothing but a headache. They might make you jump through all sorts of hoops just to have your group mentioned in the guidebook that's sent to freshmen, or make it difficult for you to poster or perform on campus. They'll make you fill out countless forms to hold a public event, and they'll force you to pay for a university police officer to monitor the cash box at your concert where you'll charge $1 admission. At times, it could feel like they're working against your interests rather than for them.

Mike's Corner

My college a cappella group encountered some problems with a dean who had a personal dislike for the sort of music we sang. He would make it difficult for us to perform at the larger campus venues, and was generally just a big obstacle we had to go through. However, we made active efforts to win his favor—such as by personally inviting him to our concerts and giving him free tickets—and after a while, we got on his good side and he dealt with us more amiably.

Nevertheless, some things your organization will want to do will require interaction with at least some members of the faculty or university administration, so try to be as nice as possible when dealing with them.

In addition to receiving help from the administration, you should ask members of the faculty who are specially trained in subjects related to your group's purpose to serve as your academic advisors. For example, a member of the art faculty might be able to give your photography journal staff some advice, and a communications professor might give pointers for your newspaper. It doesn't hurt to ask for their help, and they'll probably be flattered that you sought their expertise in the first place.

After You're Gone

Just as if you were managing your own business, you have to constantly check the pulse of your group to make sure that it's running as smoothly as possible, that you're working on things that you care about, and that the other members are enthused and excited about what they're doing. Always keep your eyes and mind open, and don't forget to ask for input from others.

Here are a few things to consider as your group grows and prospers:

✓ Is there too much organization and bureaucracy? Do you have two vice presidents and three editors who're constantly stepping on each other's toes and bickering instead of getting things done?

✓ Is there too little organization? Is publicity suffering because no one has that as their responsibility?

✓ How did the last event/issue/concert/protest go? What could you improve to make the next one better?

✓ Is your group fulfilling its mission or have you changed course? It's completely fine to go in a different direction from what you initially intended—this happens more often than you might think—and you just have to make sure that all of the processes and organization that you set up to accomplish the original goals still work.

If you're ready to start thinking about the long-term survival of your group, make sure to work out plans for the next set of officer elections, auditions, or whatever is relevant. For example, in addition to setting the date, figure out how elections will take place. Will candidates give speeches, write essays, sing, dance, or do something completely different? Who from your current group will judge new applicants, what will be the criteria, and will the vote take place as a discussion or via a more formal procedure? While these may seem like trivial issues at first, emotions can run high at elections and auditions, and everything will go more smoothly if you decide up front how things will get done.

Whether you hold official elections or not, it's important to always recruit new members into your group. Upperclassmen graduate and you need new minds and hearts to continue to make your group a success. Make sure to continue to publicize your group and its goals, take part in activity fairs, and make yourself visible to incoming freshmen who're always up for trying something new.

Also, try contacting other student groups to put on events together. For instance, it's not uncommon for an a cappella group to perform with an improv troupe, or for different dance troupes to perform together. Sometimes, a community service organization will work with a social activism group on a project, or different cultural groups will work together to put on an awesome showcase.

Teaming up with other groups is a great way to get a lot of manpower working toward your common goal. You'll find that interacting with fresh faces might invigorate the creativity of your organization and putting on a show with more performance groups will draw a larger audience (if for no other reason than because there will be more roommates obliged to attend).

6

Nailing Down Your Major

Try to put your decision off as long as you can, so that you know as much as possible.

—Junior
Harvard University

As soon as you start college, you're going to feel it: The pressure coming in from all directions, the pressure to choose a major and stick to it. Whatever you do, try to resist that pressure for as long as you can. Contrary to popular belief, you *do* have some time (usually at least three full semesters) in which to explore potential fields and take interesting courses. It helps to know from day one what you want to do for the rest of your life, but it's not necessary or likely. Spend your first one or two years exploring your interests and the academic fields you might like to study in depth.

There will naturally come a day when you do have to make a decision, but if you've followed even some of the advice in this guide, you'll be well prepared. Take a breath and dive into it, as you keep in mind the following points.

- Can I See the Menu Again?
- Double or Nothing
- Your Own Creation
- Minor League
- And the Winner Is . . .

Can I See the Menu Again?

Once you've taken a few introductory and midlevel courses, talked with a few professors and advisors, and thought long and hard about your own interests, you'll have a much better idea of where you want to go. Think about the classes you've taken so far. Which were your favorites? Was there ever a point at which you were genuinely excited by the things you were studying? If you take the time and consider your experiences, you'll probably find it relatively easy to narrow down your choices to one or two academic fields. If you can narrow it down to one, more power to you.

The key here, of course, is that you've done a little (or a lot of) research. If you haven't looked around too much and the deadline for choosing a major approaches, you may have to make an uninformed decision. If you've looked around but don't know what to do with the information you've gathered, try writing it down on paper. Sometimes when we

Julio's Corner

Below is a template that I used to help me make up my mind about a major. You don't have to use it, but it might help structure your thoughts.

Feel free to make up your own systems but here's one way to organize your thoughts on a possible major and make your task of choosing which one to make your home for the next few years a bit easier.

Major	Level of Interest	Quality of Courses	Professors and Advisors
Sociology	High	Pretty good intro class; Interesting advanced courses	Intro prof was okay; Dept. head seems great

write things down, they become much clearer in our minds, and that's the goal here. Write down some of the advantages and disadvantages of each field you're considering and include any particular features that stand out in your mind—how friendly the department head was when you approached him or her, how boring you found that 500-person intro class, and so on.

We Talk With . . .

Daniel, Senior, Castleton State College

What advice would you offer to college students about choosing a major?
If you know in your gut that your major just has to be agricultural philosophy, then go with it. If you don't know, then embrace the unknown. These years are driven by exploration and investigation, so enjoy the trip.

How did you decide on your major?
I've always been drawn to what I love. I loved the idea of being financially successful with my creativity, so I chose the major that would open up those doors—electronic business.

What was the most helpful resource for you when choosing your major?
The Internet. You can browse sites for almost every college and learn a ton about what majors they offer and what those majors are like. Surf till it hits you.

Double or Nothing

If you're lucky enough to find not one passion but two—if you find yourself torn between two possible majors, both tugging at you with the same intensity and both filled with interesting and engaging classes—then perhaps it's time to think about a double major. Before you take this leap, though, there are a few important considerations that you need to keep in mind.

First, a double major can be very, very hard. You *will* be doing more work than your single-major classmates, and that extra work will start to take its toll after a couple of years. As your classes become more and more advanced, you'll find it harder to keep up with your coursework while maintaining a reasonable social and extracurricular life. And you'll have very few credits with which to explore other academic fields.

On the plus side, double majoring allows you to explore two potentially very different academic fields in reasonable depth. You'll truly be maximizing your college education if you can handle it. A double major leaves you more options for specializing in a certain field and pursuing graduate studies in it. It also looks quite impressive on a résumé (but, of course, only if it's accompanied by a strong grade-point average).

Double majoring in Italian and international studies has really allowed me to take a wide range of classes that have really challenged me and opened my mind to so many new ideas. I could not be happier with my classes, professors, and school, which all seem to work together to provide me the best possible educational experience. With these two majors I take quite a range of courses in a few different areas, so there is always something new and interesting to learn, while still following a field I'm passionate about. Unfortunately, I don't think there is an easy or right way to choose a major. For me the best way to go about it was trial and error; originally, I started off on a completely different track and changed my mind entirely when I took some elective courses. This worked out well, because in the end I was able to confidently make a decision I knew I would be happy with, because I had already sampled so many areas. Additionally, I think when you take classes in different fields that may not be as appealing to you, you really gain appreciation for your own specialization.

—Junior
Boston College

If you do choose to double major and later find that it wasn't a wise decision, you'll probably have the option to drop one of the fields in favor of the other. Find out what the deadlines and requirements for such decisions are, and keep them in mind. You should also talk to a few double majors about their experiences. Try to find a few terrible experiences along with a few who give you wholehearted recommendations, so you can learn from both sides.

Your Own Creation

As far as I know, no one's ever done what I'm doing. That makes me feel just a little bit cooler.

—Sophomore
Rutgers University

If you're feeling extremely adventurous, or if there doesn't seem to be anything in your school's course listings to match your freewheeling spirit, then you might just be a candidate for that rarest of all majors—the self-designed program. We must warn you, however: This option is *not* for the faint of heart. It requires a tremendous degree of focus, discipline, and commitment, and, perhaps most of all, the ability to drive and push yourself.

The first thing you should do is find out your school's particular approach to self-designed majors:

✓ Who will be your academic advisor—can you choose, or is one assigned to you?
✓ How many credits will you need in order to graduate?
✓ What about a thesis and honors—who will advise and evaluate your efforts?

Think about these sorts of questions now, before you commit yourself to anything specific. You should also remember the potential advantages of being in a specific department. By choosing an established major, you become part of an academic community, one with a well-developed support system and a proven approach to study. There is much to be said for this sort of environment, and you should think long and hard before giving it up. Will you be able to find or create this type of a community with your self-designed major?

Above all, get a ton of advice: from students who've pursued their own majors, from professors who share your particular interests, and from advisors who can help you sort the practical issues. Make sure you know exactly what you're getting yourself into.

Minor League

Depending on your school, you might be able to choose a minor along with your major. Even if you don't have this option, you can select an unofficial minor by spending some of your electives on a field that interests you. Think of a minor as your secondary field of interest and focus—it will make up the second-largest group of courses in your schedule, and you'll have the chance to explore it in considerable depth.

If you're interested in two academic fields but don't think that a double major is for you, then see if you can make one of them your minor. Find out if there are specific requirements for officially designating a minor and forge ahead.

Also give some thought to the concentration you can choose within your major. For example, history is a pretty broad field. Perhaps you'll want to concentrate on a particular world region, time period, or even a particular event. You don't have to know what your concentration will be when you first choose your major, but it's something to consider as you begin your class selections.

We Talk With . . .
Megan, Senior, Middlebury College

What is your major? Are you happy with it?
My major is English and I guess that I'm happy with it. I wish that I had thought to do a double English and Italian major

earlier so that it would've been possible, but I didn't. So I have to just settle for an English major and Italian minor.

Why did you decide to choose your particular major?
I love books, I love reading, and I love writing and words. It seemed to fit. I was good at it and hated math and though I liked science, I didn't like being in labs. I liked languages but I thought that my only option as an Italian major would be to teach it and I didn't think that was what I wanted to do. Sometimes I wish that I had chosen something different, but I chose English because it makes me happy and it's something that comes to me naturally.

What was most helpful in your process of deciding on your major?
I knew that I wanted to be an English major since the beginning of high school. I never really questioned it, so I guess I didn't really turn to anyone to discuss my major because it never occurred to me to do anything else.

Do you wish that you'd done something differently when choosing your major?
I wish I had thought of doing a double or joint major.

What advice would you offer to other college students about choosing a major?
Think about what you really want to do and if you're not sure, shop around when you still can in your first year.

And the Winner Is . . .

I had to choose a major halfway through sophomore year. It was pretty ugly, but I knew that it wasn't a lifelong commitment.

—Junior
Cornell University

At some point—probably around the middle of your sophomore year—you'll have to buckle down and choose a major (or two). No matter how much research you've done, this decision will probably feel a little scary. It's kind of like considering a marriage proposal: Sure you're in love, but is he or she really the *one*?

Take a deep breath. Follow your gut instincts. Trust your judgment.

 Julio's Corner

I finally chose history and literature as my major after looking over endless lists of requirements. I'm the kind of person who can't take fifteen classes on the same subject, so I looked for fields that offered a lot of variety and weren't very pushy about specializing. In the end, I settled for studying the entire canon of Western civilization and learning its complete history. It doesn't get much broader than that.

Ten Ways Not to Choose a Major

In the spirit of knowing what you don't want to do, here are some ideas for why you should *not* choose a particular major.

1. Your parents told you that you have to major in it.
2. Your older brother or sister majored in it.
3. Many of your friends are majoring in it.
4. This major seems to have too many challenging professors and classes.
5. When you started college, you said you were going to choose this major and you feel that you should stick with your plan.
6. This major seems to have very easy requirements for graduation.
7. It has the most non–9:00 am classes.
8. A guy or a girl you have a crush on is choosing this major.
9. You picked this major out of a hat.
10. You have no idea what else you want your major to be.

Changing Your Mind

I felt like I was swimming in a current, being pushed in a certain direction day after day. I'm not sure what happened, but all of a sudden I was somewhere I didn't want to be.

—Sophomore
University of Florida

It happens all the time. You've been studying a field for a year, two years, and coasting happily along. Then it hits you: You hate what you're doing. It seemed great at first, but suddenly your classes are lethally boring, your bookshelves are lined with uninteresting books, and you can't remember the last time you had half an ounce of fun. With each passing day, you begin to wonder more and more whether you made a mistake.

First of all, relax. This sort of thing happens, and it will continue to happen as long as colleges and students coexist. The first question you should ask yourself is: Why am I so unhappy? Is it the field itself, the professors, the require-ments? Is it the school?

If the problem seems to be with your chosen major—despite your best efforts to find a good one—then allow your-self to consider the possibility of switching to something different. It's okay to change your mind, even after a couple of years. Don't let yourself get stuck with something you don't enjoy—your time is way too valuable.

Here are a few steps to follow when you think you may want to change your major.

- Nail Down the Diagnosis
- It's (Almost) Never Too Late to Change
- Take Care of Business

Nail Down the Diagnosis

After about a year of history, I realized that I couldn't take any more research paper assignments. I never seemed to be learn-ing anything useful or interesting. I was digging up obscure facts about incidents that no one cares about. I finally had to ask myself, "What's the point?" When I couldn't come up with an answer, I knew it was time to think about changing my major.

—Sophomore
Harvard University

The first thing you should do is try to pinpoint the source of the problem. What is it that you dislike about your field? Is there something else you'd rather be doing? Questions like these can help you define your unhappiness in more useful terms. Don't immediately assume that the problem is with you, that you simply don't belong in college, or that you're incapable of liking academics. You probably just haven't found something that genuinely interests you. And in that you're definitely not alone.

One of the best ways to locate the source of trouble is to look over your grades for the last couple of years. In which classes did you do best and worst? A good grade is often an indication of extra effort on your part, and extra effort is often a sign of personal interest. Pay particular attention to poor grades in courses that you *had* to take because of your major but wouldn't have taken if it were your choice. These can often speak volumes about your interests and the conflicts you might be having with your field of study.

It's (Almost) Never Too Late to Change

I just couldn't get through my requirements because I hated chemistry so much. I thought I was going to die, and then I realized that I wouldn't have to take organic chemistry if I changed my major a little.

—Junior
University of Rhode Island

Once you have a solid enough understanding of the issues you have with your major you can look for ways to correct it. If you hate your field's requirements, look for a field with looser or more agreeable guidelines. If you can't stand the particular method by which your field is studied, look for a field that studies something in a different way. If you're simply bored with what you're studying, look for something more interesting (easier said than done, of course, but you *can* do it).

Choosing a major becomes progressively easier as you spend more time in college—you learn more about yourself and your interests with each passing day. By your second or third year, you've taken a few courses and (hopefully) considered a few fields. Bring this experience into the equation. What were some of your favorite classes? Was there ever an assignment that you *didn't* hate doing, and if so, what made this assignment more enjoyable than most? These kinds of questions, along with the kinds of inquiries you might have made when choosing your major in the first place, will help you find a new line of study.

Changing your major can be a stressful and frustrating experience. But try to keep in mind that you're capable of getting through it and making your college experience more enjoyable in the process. You know exactly what you need to do: Think about what bothers you and what interests you, talk to a few advisors and professors, and make a decision. Follow your instincts and, above all, *trust yourself*. Ignore for a few moments the pressure you're probably feeling and let your own beliefs rule.

The Art World

by Victoria, Sophomore,
Pratt Institute

My major is graphic design, and I'm definitely happy with the choice I made although it's tough to say considering I only just finished foundation year (art school starts with a foundation year which gives you a broad sense of the arts in all media and then second year you actually start your major). Anyway, I am happy I chose it because it's what I like to do. Creating images with computers comes naturally to me. It's also a pretty promising career in the art world, but then again almost any art-related major can be promising, it's really just up to the person to make that happen. You can make a career in art! Don't let anyone tell you otherwise (not even your parents!!!).

I didn't know what I wanted to do in high school. I knew it would deal with design, so naturally I leaned toward a more structured course as opposed to just plain fine arts. When choosing my major I definitely wish I did things differently. I wish that my teachers and school had provided me with more information on the many art careers that there are in the world. I wish I had taken a pre-college course to see what was out there.

Even though I could've changed my major this year, I chose not to. But the first year definitely sparked lots of things inside me that I wish would've happened to me a year or two earlier. I would say this to students interested in the performing and fine-arts fields: If your high school does not specialize in these areas, *definitely* seek outside learning. It will really open your eyes and give you a different perspective on things. And even if you're not sure, it's okay because you always have freshman year to figure things out.

Take Care of Business

Once you've chosen a new field, you'll quickly have to deal with a few practical considerations. The most important, of course, are graduation and major requirements. Do you have enough time to complete the required courses for your new major? If you're a junior or senior, you'll have fewer options. Many schools limit the number of terms you can attend and federal financial aid only covers eight semesters. Because some schools also have strict requirements for particular disciplines, your only choice might be a field similar to the one you're pursuing or one that has many similar requirements.

If you're not sure about your requirements, take the time to talk to an advisor within the new department and develop a plan of study. If all the practical issues are stacked against you, it may be impossible to change your field significantly. Even in this situation, you should still consider minor alterations to your track:

✓ Can you refocus on a different historical time period?
✓ Can you study French literature rather than French linguistics?
✓ Can you switch from microeconomics to macro?

You might find that making a change within your major will make you happier and more academically satisfied. It's definitely worth the effort.

8

Idea Generators

Sometimes we all need a little push to get our brain cells flowing in the right direction. Choosing a major is one of those moments—you might know what you need to do to nail down your choice, but just need a little something to get started with this often-intimidating process. In this chapter we've put together a few pages of idea generators, as we like to call them. We've highlighted a few general areas of interests that you might have and have included suggestions for what majors you might consider and what careers you might think about after graduation.

By no means have we covered every interest or every possible major and career choice. But our goal here is to get you thinking in the right direction and make your major selection just a bit less intimidating. Check it out!

If you're interested in the media . . .

check out these majors . . .

Communications	Film
Comparative literature	Fine arts
English	History
Journalism	Journalism
Creative writing	Sociology

. . . and these careers

Newspaper/Magazine publishing

Publisher	Copy editor
Editor	Layout designer
Columnist	Online columnist
Reporter	Ad manager

Book publishing

Publisher	Agent
Editor	Layout designer
Author	Copy editor
Publicist	Marketing manager

Radio/TV/Movies

Program director	Actor
Director	Anchor
Producer	Cameraman

Reporter   Disc jockey
Screenwriter   Talk show host

Music industry

Record company exec   Agent
Record producer   Publicist
Marketing manager

We Talk With . . .

Nicole, Sophomore,
New York University

What is your major? Are you happy with it? Why?
I've decided to major in film and television production. I love the classes and the talented people I've met and will probably work with in the future. I have never been the student who excelled in math or science so I needed a major that let me explore my creativity. In film and tv, there are so many different job opportunities to look into after you graduate. I like the feeling of not having to settle on anything right now, like accounting or teaching.

Why did you decide to choose your particular major?
I kind of got thrown into it. It started in my sophomore year of high school when my best friend had entered a contest for Showtime where he had to write a treatment and if chosen, film it. Since his original actress had gotten sick, he asked me to star in it. I realized I was much more comfortable behind the camera than in front of it. We took a summer film class together and I really enjoyed it. Then in junior year, I passed by a poster for New York University's Future Filmmakers Workshop, where I decided to apply for the hell of it. Around the same time, I also

entered the Showtime contest. Much to my surprise, I got called back for both. Although I was not chosen as a finalist for Showtime, I was one of the fifteen students accepted into the [free] workshop held on Saturdays, 9-5, from February to May. I realized it was a lot of fun and you can do so much with film and television such as entertain an audience or use it as a way to spread political awareness.

If you're interested in performance art:

check out these majors . . .

Communications

English

Fine arts

Art history

Music

Theater studies

Theater management

Acting

Dance

Film

. . . and these careers
Theater

Theater manager

Actor

Director

Producer

Program director

Set designer

Costume designer

Music

Pop singer

Opera singer

Composer

Film score composer

Orchestra member   Radio jingle composer
Orchestra director   Music teacher

Dance

Dancer   Costume designer
Set designer   Show producer
Director   Dance group manager

We Talk With . . .

Jayme, Sophomore,
New York University–Tisch

What is your major? Are you happy with it?
I am a theater/drama major and will be double majoring in psychology. I am extremely happy with my choice in major.

Why did you decide to choose your particular major?
There was never really a question in my mind as to whether or not I would be studying theater in college. I have been acting since I was very young, and have found it to be what makes me the happiest. I could never see myself doing anything else. I chose psychology as my second major after I took introduction to psychology. I enjoyed the class and really connected with the material. I knew when I enjoyed reading a textbook that this would be a good choice of double major for me.

What was most helpful in your process of deciding on your major?
For theater, it was something I just always knew I would do because I wanted to. I knew what I wanted to do with my life and what made me happy and so I picked to study that. I think that

students need to find out who they are and what fulfills their lives and study things they are interested in. That doesn't work for everyone, but in truth the people I see who work jobs for the money alone aren't as happy as those who work because they love it. It's the same thing with studying in school.

Do you wish that you'd done something differently when choosing your major?
Not a thing. Maybe in a year I'll want to switch, but that's okay. College is about finding who you are and what you like. There's room for mistakes; everyone's only human, flaws and all.

What advice would you offer to other college students about choosing a major?
Find something that makes *you* happy, not anyone else. Think of what you want to do with your life when you graduate. Figure out what would make you happy in a perfect world and then find the closest realistic thing to that. By the time you have to commit yourself to a field, you'll hopefully have a reasonable idea of what you want to do. Take a last look through your notes, think for a bit, and make what you feel to be the best decision. It's not too terrible a moment—deep down, you probably know what the answer is. And whatever you choose, remember that it's not forever and that your college major will probably not define the rest of your life.

If you're interested in serving the community:

check out these majors . . .

Anthropology   International studies
Sociology   Religion

Psychology	Philosophy
Ethnic studies	Women's studies
History	Latin American/African American studies

. . . and these careers
Social work

Social worker	Counselor
Family services worker	Community organizer
Community educator	Educator

Nonprofit management

Director of nonprofit	Grant writer
Foundation director	Policy director
Think-tank director	Government liaison

Other

Peace Corps volunteer	Writer
Teach for America member	Researcher
Cultural group director	Youth mentor

If you're interested in politics:

check out these majors . . .

| Government | Sociology |
| Political science | Pre-Law |

History
Economics
Philosophy

Public policy
Urban planning
Anthropology

. . . and these careers
Government

Governor
Mayor
Congressman
Senator
Speech writer
Campaign manager
Lobbyist

Policy advisor
Staff member of CIA/FBI
United Nations representative
Diplomat
Member of foreign service

Social Activism

Grass roots organizer
Educator

Nonprofit director
Lobbyist

Other

Member of a think tank
Policy researcher

Political writer
Professor

If you're interested in technology . . .

check out these majors . . .

Computer engineering
Computer science

Technology and society
Telecommunications

Computer networking

Systems security

Construction technologies

Biotechnology

Technical education

Web/Multimedia

. . . and these careers

Computer science

Programmer

Hardware developer

Software developer

Database administrator

Tech support

Technical writer

Chief technical officer

Networking

Network administrator

Tech analyst

Quality control manager

Network architect

Systems analyst

IT manager

IT security

Field engineer

Internet

Web designer

Project manager

Information architect

E-commerce consultant

Web developer

Biotechnology

Lab technician

Research consultant

Biostatistics engineer

Manufacturing technician

Bioinformatics developer

Scientific technician

Marketing analyst/Associate

If you're interested in business . . .

check out these majors . . .

Business management
Small business
administration
Business writing
Business/Managerial
economics
Marketing

Arts management
Accounting

Micro- or macroeconomics

Retail management

. . . and these careers

Finance

Accountant
Investment banker
Venture capitalist
Stockbroker
Financial advisor

Management consultant
Fund accountant
Research analyst
Portfolio manager

Insurance

Actuary
Agent or broker
Claims adjuster
Service representative

Loss-control specialist
Risk manager
Underwriter

Accounting

Staff and senior audit

Management accountant

accountants   Internal auditor
Staff tax accountant

Entrepreneur

Self-employed   Corporate trainer
Small-business owner   Independent consultant

We Talk With . . .

Ryan, Recent Grad, University of
Wisconsin–Oshkosh and Whitewater

What was your major? Were you happy with it?
I began with a major in human resources management when I
started my college path. However, I soon realized that a lot of
the coursework in human resources lacked the personal aspect,
which is very important to a well-rounded human resources professional. I decided that in order to be more marketable, I would
add a communications degree to my college curriculum. So, I
ended up graduating with two degrees. I was very happy with
the decision that I made. I picked majors that are very well-
rounded and that prepared me for a career in human resources.

Why did you decide to choose your particular major?
I think it all started with my particular interest as a kid in wanting
to be a teacher. At first I wanted to teach high school, then I
thought about college. I quickly realized, however, just how little
respect people in those positions have. I would see how other
student's parents tried to bully teachers into doing what they
wanted, whether that be giving their children better grades
(however undeserved) or into changing their teaching methods. I

really felt that with my strong will, I would not do well in a pro-fession where such a large population was critiquing my every move. I always had a good business sense, so I started looking into business classes. All through high school, I took as many busi-ness electives as I could and soon found a niche in my manage-ment and personnel classes. I enjoyed the mentoring, coaching, training, and development aspects that were associated with the human resources profession and found myself craving more infor-mation. One of my business teachers had attended the University of Wisconsin–Whitewater and got me interested in going to school there. I researched their HR program and found it to be one of the best. From there, things just fell into place.

What was most helpful in your process of deciding on your major?

It would definitely be the coursework I took in high school. Knowing that I wanted a career in business, I took as many business classes as I could to find out more about the different aspects of business. I quickly learned that I disliked account-ing (too many numbers) but found the people side of things to be much more interesting. Human resources was right up my alley.

Do you wish that you'd done something differently when choosing your major?

I wish I would've researched colleges a little better and looked at which ones had the best technology and would have given me the best background in human resources so that I could have come out of college with more knowledge about the field. I came out of college with an opportunity to jump into an entry-level HR position that was a generalist role. Those are very hard to find and very difficult for someone to fill right out of college because many aspects of HR are learned on the job. It's hard to teach someone to deal with the variety of issues that could come up on any given day. There probably needs to be more hands-on experience with a college program in HR.

What advice would you offer to other college students about choosing a major?
Pick a major based on what classes you enjoy taking. You don't have to stick with one major, but only taking your general education credits, waiting to pick a major does you no good. There are many 100-level courses that serve as a great introduction to different majors. Take some of those to see which one(s) spark some interest for you. Then follow that path. You are always going to have to take some classes along that path that are not going to interest you, but stick with it. Some of those classes are simply used as a method to weed out students who are afraid of doing a little extra work to get what they want.

If you're interested in education . . .

check out these majors . . .

Education

Special education

Speech pathology

Urban education

Teacher education

Early childhood development

English/Writing

Social studies education

Technical education

. . . and these careers
Secondary education

Public school teacher

Private school teacher

Guidance counselor

Principal

College counselor   Librarian
Private tutor

Higher education

College professor   Academic coach
Admissions director   Student recruiter
School/Class dean

Education management

E-learning specialist   Technology consultant
Curriculum developer

Specialized

Child care   Nurse educator
Foreign language instructor Test Center educator
Wilderness youth instructor Technical instructor
Music teacher

We Talk With . . .

Rebecca, Recent Grad,
University of Wisconsin–Madison

What was your major? Were you happy with it?

I majored in education, more specifically, special education.
I'm very happy that I majored in this subject because I hold
a special passion for it—it's something that I enjoy and

thrive on. And of course, it's also a very easy major to get a job in.

Why did you decide to choose your particular major?

I wanted to be a teacher since third grade. It wasn't until I started working with individuals with disabilities when I was a sophomore in high school that I thought about teaching students with disabilities. I volunteered through my church and taught classes at sixteen. I found it extremely rewarding to myself and those who I worked with.

Do you wish that you'd done something differently when choosing your major?

No, knowing what I wanted to go into wasn't hard. However, I should've started learning the requirements of my major in advance. I should have talked with a guidance counselor more often because I was hard-pressed to graduate in four years. I did it, but not without three summer classes that could have possibly been avoided had I taken the classes I needed starting out.

What advice would you offer to other college students about choosing a major?

Follow your heart, and then explore the options that use the things that interest you. There is more than one major that may be appropriate for you and that you find interesting. Explore them and then decide which fits you and your personality best. However, *don't waste time*. You won't be in college forever (unless, of course, you never decide a major).

If you're interested in science . . .

check out these majors . . .

Biology	Science technologies
Biochemistry	Biotechnology
Sociology	Engineering
Seismology	Nutritional sciences
Geophysics	Molecular sciences

. . . and these careers

Research

Geneticist	Ecologist
Physicist	Oncologist
Chemist	Botanist

Biotechnology

Lab technician	Quality control analyst
Research associate	Clinical research physician
Research scientist	

Support

Medical researcher	Computer scientist
Lab manager	Sales and marketing
Lab technician	Diagnostician

Mechanical Engineering

by Joseph, Senior, Brown University

I'm a mechanical engineering major with a more specific focus on engineering mechanics. Until very recently I was focusing on engineering systems design, but because of the fact that I'm considering continuing my education into a graduate-level program, engineering mechanics made much more sense.

By and large I'm pretty happy with my major. The broad science curriculum fits my interests very well as I was always much more interested in science that humanities. While I knew that I wanted to study a hard science, I really had no idea of which one. Engineering has basically enabled me to study a variety of sciences in depth. I do often get frustrated with some of the engineering classes even though I find them interesting. Most of the faculty are interested and excited about teaching, but this enthusiasm does not always make them good instructors. Some of the lab activities required for these courses can also be so unorganized and hackneyed as to make them basically useless. Having said that, now that I'm taking mostly upper-level courses, which tend to be much smaller, these problems no longer bother me.

If you're interested in medicine . . .

check out these majors . . .

Pre-Medicine
Biology
Nursing

Anatomy
Biomedical engineering
Clinical medicine

Pharmacology   Psychotherapy
Genetic counseling

. . . and these careers
Physician

Primary care physician   Neurologist
Plastic surgeon   Anesthesiologist
Cardiologist   Radiologist
Emergency medicine

Nursing

Registered nurse   Physical therapist
Licensed practical nurse   Home health care
Nurse practitioner   Long-term care nurse

Support/Specialist

Medical technician   Health care management
Medical secretary   Drug lab administrator
Genetic counselor   Lab manager
Lab technologist

Pharmaceuticals

Pharmacist   Pharmaceutical sales
Pharmacy technician   Clinical pharmacist
Research chemist   Pharmacy manager

If you're interested in the humanities . . .

check out these majors . . .

English   Social psychology
Philosophy   Foreign language studies
History   Musicology
Art history   Theater
Film studies

. . . and these careers
Journalism and Publishing

Reporter   Editor
Specialized writer   Copy editor
Broadcasting   Publisher
Public relations

Education

Teacher   Guidance counselor
College professor   Curriculum developer
Social worker

Nonprofit and Government

Executive director   Press secretary
Program director   Foreign service officer
Development and
Legislative aide

fund-raising
Event coordinator
Director of volunteers

Environmental protection
specialist
Intelligence analyst

Entertainment and the Arts

TV/Film writer
Producer
Performer
Film editor

Director
Stage manager
Museum curator

Law

Firm associate
In-house associate counsel
Public defender

Legal-aid lawyer
Nonprofit attorney
Paralegal

We Talk With . . .

Pam, Recent Grad, University of
Wisconsin–Whitewater

What was your major? Were you happy with it?
I majored in philosophy, and I am really happy with my decision to
do so because it was very challenging, and it kept me on my toes.
Also, in retrospect, it taught me a lot about logical thinking—a
skill that I've been able to apply in real life after school.

Why did you decide to choose your particular major?
Philosophy was much different and more academic than anything I had studied or been involved with prior to choosing it
as a major.

What was most helpful in your process of deciding on your major?

A mixture of talking to other students in the department, taking the introductory courses offered by the program, as well as meeting and talking with the professors who taught those courses.

Do you wish that you'd done something differently when choosing your major?

I wish I'd explored more aspects of the program, both academic and extracurricular, beyond just the core graduation requirements.

What advice would you offer to other college students about choosing a major?

Don't choose your major solely based on what you know or are familiar with. Be receptive to new ideas and pick something that is both interesting to you as well as challenging.

Adults Weigh In

We asked a few professors and advisors from Davidson, Harvard, Princeton, Stanford, and the University of Michigan to share their wisdom on major selection. Here's what they had to say.

What Would You Say to a Student Trying to Choose a Major?

Look hard and long. Don't get stuck doing what you think you should be doing. College is expensive. Make the best of it.

Shop, shop, shop, and don't get distracted by clearance sales and fancy banners. The best majors are usually the little ones, the ones with dusty old professors and magical books lurking in ancient bookshelves.

Talk to everyone you know and write down their advice.

Find a good advisor and stick to him or her. They'll help you immensely.

Use the Internet whenever possible. You can get more research done online in a couple of hours than in a whole day of trekking. Every department will probably have a website, and every website will have at least some useful information. Read as much as you can, but make sure you pay a physical visit to the department if you have any unanswered questions.

To What Extent Should Students Consider Their Careers When Choosing a Major?

I don't think college is the place, at least initially, to decide the course of your life. College is the place to obtain a liberal arts education, to round yourself out as a human being.

You'll have time to think about that later. Your first couple of years, you shouldn't even know your favorite ice cream flavor, let alone the career you should pursue. Let your experiences guide your choices, and keep an eye out for the really cool jobs.

There are certain considerations you should keep in mind when choosing a major and one of them is undoubtedly your career. If you want to be a doctor or lawyer, you have to take steps early to meet requirements. Keep your options open, though. Look around as much as your track will allow and you might discover something unexpected.

You should do what you *love*. Getting a job is easy. Getting a job you like requires that you have some experience in listening to yourself.

When Should a Student Decide on a Major?

I'd say around the end of sophomore year. Even if your school makes you do it earlier, you can just fudge that and choose your real major later.

The decision should take place in several steps. Narrow your choices from four or five to two or three and down to one. You should probably make it to the end of that ladder by the last couple of months of your sophomore year. There might be time to step back later, but you have to make a commitment.

Whenever you find something you really love. It might take a month, it might take four years. If you need to spend eight years in college to find something you like, then that's how long you should be there. If that's not possible at your school, go someplace else.

Helpful Resources

We spent a bit of time looking for some helpful books and we found a few that you might find useful. Remember that your own college or university probably has many great resources—booklets, websites, etc.—to help you think through your options. Take advantage of them. You have to make your own decisions, but that doesn't mean you have to make them in isolation.

Major in Success: Make College Easier, Fire Up Your Dreams, and Get a Very Cool Job, by Patrick Combs and Jack Canfield. Ten Speed Press, 3rd Edition, April 2000.

A high-energy book to help you discover your interests, passions, career, and life goals. It's written by a not-so-long-ago grad, and we think you'll appreciate the peer perspective.

What Every College Student Should Know: How to Find the Best Teachers and Learn the Most from Them, by Ernie

Lepore and Sarah-Jane Leslie. Rutgers University Press, March 2002.

This concise and efficient little book will help you with seeking out the best professors and the most interesting classes, which will give you a slight edge in your major-hunting process.

The College Majors Handbook: The Actual Jobs, Earnings, and Trends for Graduates of 60 College Majors, by Paul E. Harrington, Thomas F. Harrington, and Neeta P. Fogg. Jist Works, January 1999.

While we've harped on the fact that your major doesn't have to be connected to a particular career, you might find it helpful to learn about your options. There aren't enough truly useful books on this subject, but this one can give you a pretty good overview of what students with certain majors have gone on to do in their lives.

McGraw-Hill publishes a whole series of books with career ideas for various majors. They're titled *Great Jobs for English Majors, Great Jobs for Psychology Majors,* and so on. You might find them useful as you ponder your major selection. Nearly all are available online, and they won't set you back more than eleven or twelve dollars.

The following websites are portals for college students that offer various articles and discussion boards on topics such as participating in extracurriculars. They are great places to ask questions to a community of students from other universities with diverse perspectives:

www.collegeclub.com
www.student.com
www.campusnut.com

The Final Word

We're all afraid of making mistakes—life sometimes seems to be an endless series of opportunities to mess up. The last bit of advice we can give you is this: *Don't be afraid*. Life is short, college is shorter, and your only responsibility is to get the most out of what you're given. Choosing the right major is one giant step in that direction.

Doctors say that the best way to keep your mind strong and alert is to do something new every day. As the four years of college fly past you (and, oh, how the years *do* fly), make sure to hold on to your sense of adventure. Never let yourself fall into doing the expected or the ordinary. Instead, take a chance, venture into unfamiliar fields, and surprise yourself. If you don't like what you're learning, change it. What do you have to lose?

However scary this might sound, you're in control of your own destiny. Make it one that makes you happy.

To learn more about Students Helping Students® books, read samples and student-written articles, share your own experiences with other students, suggest a topic, or ask questions, visit us at www.StudentsHelpingStudents.com!

We're always looking for fresh minds and new ideas!

Index